Globetrotter™

Travel Guide

MADEIRA

CHRISTOPHER AND MELANIE RICE

NEW HOLLAND

- ★★★ Highly recommended
- ★★ Recommended
- ★ See if you can

Third edition published in 2009
by New Holland Publishers (UK) Ltd
London • Cape Town • Sydney • Auckland

10 9 8 7 6 5 4 3 2 1

website: www.newhollandpublishers.com

Garfield House, 86 Edgware Road
London W2 2EA,
United Kingdom

80 McKenzie Street
Cape Town 8001,
South Africa

Unit 1, 66 Gibbes Street,
Chatswood, NSW 2067
Australia

218 Lake Road,
Northcote, Auckland,
New Zealand

Distributed in the USA by
The Globe Pequot Press, Connecticut

Copyright © 2009 in text: Christopher and Melanie Rice
Copyright © 2009 in maps: Globetrotter Travel Maps
Copyright © 2009 in photographs: Individual photographers as credited (right)
Copyright © 2009 New Holland Publishers (UK) Ltd

All rights reserved. No part of this publication may be reproduced, stored in a retrieval system or transmitted, in any form or by any means, electronic, mechanical, photocopying, recording or otherwise, without the prior written permission of the publishers and copyright holders.

ISBN 978 1 84537 862 2

This guidebook has been written by independent authors and updaters. The information therein represents their impartial opinion, and neither we nor the publishers accept payment in return for including in the book or writing more favourable reviews of any of the establishments. Whilst every effort has been made to ensure that this guidebook is as accurate and up to date as possible, please be aware that the facts quoted are subject to change, particularly the price of food, transport and accommodation. The Publisher accepts no responsibility or liability for any loss, injury or inconvenience incurred by readers or travellers using this guide.

Keep us Current
Information in travel guides is apt to change, which is why we regularly update our guides. We'd be grateful to receive feedback if you've noted something we should include in our updates. If you have new information, please share it with us by writing to the Publishing Manager, Globetrotter, at the office nearest to you (addresses on this page). The most significant contribution to each new edition will receive a free copy of the updated guide.

Publishing Manager: Thea Grobbelaar
DTP Cartographic Manager: Genené Hart
Editors: Lorissa Bouwer, Carla Zietsman, Deidré Petersen, Melany McCallum
Design and DTP: Nicole Bannister, Lellyn Creamer
Cartographers: Rudi de Lange, Reneé Spocter, Genené Hart, Lucian Packies
Consultant: Rowland Mead
Picture Researchers: Felicia Apollis, Shavonne Govender, Colleen Abrahams

Reproduction by Hirt & Carter (Pty) Ltd, Cape Town
Printed and bound by Times Offset (M) Sdn. Bhd., Malaysia.

Photographic Credits:
AA Photo Library: pages 114, 117, 120
Hutchison Library/Nigel Sitwell: pages 54, 57, 68, 84
IPB/Adrian Baker: pages 4, 32, 55
IPB/Jeanetta Baker: pages 45, 81, 83, 87, 102, 104
IPB/Peter Baker: pages 7, 26, 101
jonarnoldimages.com/Walter Bibikow: pages 18, 49
jonarnoldimages.com/Danielle Gali: page 90
Pictures Colour Library: cover, pages 8, 28, 73, 78, 103;
F. Rigaud/Travel-Images.com: page 21
Neil Setchfield: pages 11, 16, 20, 23, 25, 39, 47, 50, 92, 96, 100, 109
Jeroen Snijders: title page, pages 9, 10, 13, 17, 19, 24, 27, 29, 30, 31, 36, 37, 38, 40, 42, 43, 44, 46, 48, 52, 60, 63, 64, 65, 66, 67, 69, 70, 71, 72, 74, 75, 76, 82, 85, 86, 88, 89, 91, 93, 98, 106, 107, 110, 111, 112

(IPB: International PhotoBank)

Acknowledgements:
Christopher and Melanie Rice would like to thank Maria Luisa Perestrello of the Regional Tourist Board in Funchal for her assistance.

Cover: *A spectacular view over Funchal.*
Title page: *Madeira's relaxed and carefree atmosphere makes it the perfect place to unwind.*

CONTENTS

1. Introducing Madeira 5
　The Land 6
　History in Brief 13
　Government and Economy 23
　The People 25

2. Funchal 33
　Town Centre 34
　Harbour District 40
　Praça do Municipio 46
　Zona Velha 50
　Hotel Zone 53
　Jardim Botânico 56

3. Western Madeira 61
　Ponta do Pargo 62
　Ponta do Sol 63
　The West Coast 64
　Ribeira Brava 66
　Porto Moniz 67
　Seixal 68
　Fanal 70
　The North Coast Road 71
　São Vicente 72
　Paúl da Serra 73
　Rabaçal 74
　Boca da Encumeada 76

4. Central Madeira 79
　Câmara de Lobos 81
　Cabo Girão 83
　Curral das Freiras 84
　Monte 85
　Ribeiro Frio 88
　Pico do Arieiro 90
　Faial 91
　Santana 91
　Arco do São Jorge 93

5. Eastern Madeira 97
　Camacha 100
　Santo da Serra 101
　Portela 103
　Porto da Cruz 104
　Ponta do Garajau 105
　Caniço 105
　Santa Cruz 106
　Machico 107
　Caniçal 110
　Prainha 111
　Ponta de São Lourenço 111

6. Porto Santo 115
　Cidade Vila Baleira 115
　Ponta da Calheta 117
　Fonte da Areia 117
　A Tour of the Island 118
　Ilhas Desertas 120

Travel Tips 122

Index 127

1
Introducing Madeira

Madeira is a Portuguese island dependency in the Atlantic Ocean, about 800km (497 miles) off the coast of Africa and 1000km (621 miles) southwest of Lisbon. On the same latitude as Bermuda, the mild subtropical climate is the stuff of legend, and was an important factor in attracting the first (mainly British) tourists at the beginning of the 19th century. Madeira is small – roughly the size of Menorca – but the sheer diversity of landscape and scenery is astonishing and greater than can be found in many countries. Towering volcanic peaks, dramatic gorges, great swathes of primeval laurel forest, river valleys clad in luxuriant vegetation, terraced hillsides planted with vines and bananas, cliffs of awesome dimensions – these are just some of the contrasts Madeira offers its visitors. Flowers of every description, introduced from Asia, Africa and the Americas or native to the island, appear in profusion and are without a doubt one of its prime assets. While Madeira is mostly mountainous, exploring the less accessible regions becomes easier (and more enjoyable) once you discover the *levada* trails that crisscross the rugged terrain.

Funchal is Madeira's capital and hub. Home to nearly half the inhabitants, it's a lively town with a beautiful coastal setting and there's enough in the way of historic buildings, parks, gardens and museums to occupy most visitors for at least a few days. Those seeking a more active holiday will relish the opportunities for golf, tennis, surfing, hang-gliding, scuba diving and sea fishing in coastal resorts around the island. Madeira's unremittingly rocky

Top Attractions

*** Porto Santo: the beach to beat all beaches – 9km (5.6 miles) of golden sand.
*** Curral das Freiras: spectacular valley, on every tourist itinerary.
*** Pico do Arieiro: Madeira's third highest mountain offers the best views.
*** Monte: toboggan rides, gardens and a cable car.
*** Quinta do Palheiro Ferreiro: plants and trees from Asia, Africa and America.
** Cabo Girão: the world's fourth highest cliff.
** Adegas de São Francisco: discover Madeiran wine.

Opposite: *Folk dancers in traditional costume pose for tourists.*

> **FACTS AND FIGURES**
>
> **Population:** Madeira 241,000; Porto Santo 4400. The other islands are uninhabited. More than 40% of the population lives in the capital, Funchal. The population density on Madeira is 440 per km², one of the greatest concentrations in the European Union.
> **Government:** Autonomous Administrative Region within the Republic of Portugal.
> **Language:** Portuguese.
> **Religion:** Roman Catholic.

shoreline is an obvious drawback if you're partial to lying out on sand; but with the long, golden beach at **Porto Santo** only a ferry ride away, even this shortfall pales into insignificance. An 'imported' beach at **Calheta** on Madeira island is also a great attraction for childen.

THE LAND

Madeira originated more than 20 million years ago from a series of cataclysmic volcanic eruptions beneath the Atlantic Ocean. Successive layers of rapidly cooling lava and igneous rock built up from the seabed to raise a cone-shaped island above the surface. In this respect, Madeira resembles an immense iceberg: more than 60% of its mass is hidden underwater, at depths of up to 3600m (11,800ft). Streams of molten ash and lava continued to flow down the sides of the cone, moulding the ridge that forms the backbone of the island. This process was completed some 1.8 million years ago. Madeira's volcanoes were active for much longer, however – the last eruptions occurred around 400,000 years ago, when the magma flow created the caves of **São Vicente**.

Landscape

Madeira, then, is rugged and mountainous, nearly 50% of the terrain lying above 700m (2297ft). The highest point is **Pico Ruivo de Santana** at 1862m (6109ft). To the west of the mountain ridge is a deep, steep-sided ravine formed by the **Ribeira Brava** and the **Ribeira São Vicente** which effectively cuts the island in half, via the dramatic mountain pass at **Encumeada**. Beyond these river valleys is **Paúl da Serra**, a plateau of bleak, windswept moorland, 1400m (4593ft) above sea level. East of the central ridge the landscape becomes relatively less dramatic, as the peaks yield to gentler slopes and plateaus.

In the days of the discoverers Madeira was densely wooded and carpeted with thick vegetation. While much of the tree cover has disappeared, the valleys of the interior are still remarkably lush and hospitable, nowhere more so than **Rabaçal** with its laurel thickets, rampant ferns, cataracts and gorges. This rural idyll is a world away from the weather-worn headlands and gaunt, vertiginous cliffs of basalt and reddish tufa which make up the coastline. **Cabo Girão**, at 580m (1903ft), is the fourth highest cliff in the world. Five hundred years ago the first Portuguese settlers began cultivating the southern shoreline, which remains the most densely populated part of the island. Here every fragment of land is claimed for farming – the trademark *poios* (terraces), planted with vines, bananas, beans, maize, potatoes and other crops, a familiar feature of the Madeiran landscape.

Above: *At 580m (1903ft), Cabo Girão is the world's fourth highest cliff.*

Flora

When Madeira's first settlers set the forested island ablaze to clear land for farming, they unwittingly wiped out a priceless ecological inheritance. For this was no ordinary forest. The **laurissilva** (laurel forest), indigenous to the region, dated back to the Tertiary Era and had escaped extinction during the Ice Age, when the vegetation covering most of Europe was destroyed. Situated between 300m (984ft) and 1300m (4265ft) above sea level, the 15,000 or so hectares of laurel forest which has survived down to our own day was accorded **UNESCO World Natural Heritage** status in 1999 under the protection of the Madeira Nature Reserve. The forest contains a number of tree species, all members of the evergreen family, notably the *Lauris azorica* (bay tree), used locally in cooking, the *Vinhático*, better known as Madeiran mahogany, and the till (*Ocotea foetens*). The **dragon tree** (*Dracaeana draco*) deserves special mention. Famed for its reddish resin ('dragon's blood'), it is rarely encountered in the wild nowadays but its clusters of spear-like leaves are a familiar sight on Porto Santo.

GEOGRAPHY

Location: The Madeiran archipelago (Madeira, Porto Santo, Desertas and Selvagens) lies between latitude 32–33° north, and longtitude 16–17° west.
Area: Total surface area is 796km² (307 sq miles). Madeira is 57km (35 miles) long and 22km (14 miles) wide; Porto Santo is 11km (7 miles) long and 5km (3 miles) wide.
Highest peak: Pico Ruivo de Santana – 1862m (6109ft).
Highest cliff: Cabo Girão – 580m (1903ft).

FLOWERS IN BLOOM

• **January–March:** anemone, arum lily, camellia, camel's foot tree, cattleya, cymbidium, golden shower, mimosa, pride of Madeira, sword aloe.
• **April–June:** African flame tree, agapanthus, anemone, anthurium, camellia, cattleya, jacaranda, lupin, rhododendron, passion flower, star jasmine.
• **July–September:** agave, agapanthus, anthurium, belladonna lily, frangipani, golden trumpet, hydrangea, Madeiran orchid, Mexican dahlia, oleander, red hot poker, tears of Christ, tulip tree.
• **October–December:** belladonna lily, camellia, golden shower, golden trumpet, lady's slipper orchid, sword aloe, mimosa, poinsettia.
• **Year-round:** bougainvillea, hibiscus, honeysuckle, morning glory, strelitzia.

Of the 200 floral species endemic to Macronesia (a region which includes the Canaries, the Azores and the Cape Verde islands), around 80 are indigenous to Madeira. Most of these grow on the uplands to altitudes of about 1000m (3280ft). They include the Madeira violet, the yellow foxglove, sow thistle and native species of geranium and orchid.

If Madeira deserves the epithet 'floating garden', much of the credit must go to the British, keen amateur gardeners who exploited to the full the mild climatic conditions and rich volcanic soil. The manifests of British merchant vessels calling at Funchal read like a horticulturist's wish list of bulbs and seeds, collected from the remotest corners of the globe. Two centuries on and the legacy is plain for all to see in the towering camellia trees with their brilliant white and red-streaked flowers, the araucaria pines from Brazil, the cedars from the Atlas Mountains, the South African proteas and pink-flowered amaryllis, the Australian banksias, Japanese wisteria and Mexican frangipani. And the cornucopia is not confined to rural *quintas* and public gardens. Jacaranda trees flourish beside Funchal's busy roads, bougainvillea cling to the river embankments, while the alluring fragrance of jasmine escapes the bounds of garden walls.

Bird Life

While Madeira lies some way off the main migration route and attracts only a small variety of breeding birds, it still holds plenty of interest, not only for trained ornithologists but for keen amateur bird-watchers. The **Desertas** and **Selvagen** islands, both remote and uninhabited, are officially protected sanctuaries for sea birds like shearwaters and petrels. Closer to home, Fea's petrel has been spotted off **Porto Santo**, while Cory's shearwater sometimes makes an appearance off the coast of Madeira itself – especially around **Ponta de São Lourenço**. Balcões is another bird-watching 'hot spot', as are the São Jorge estuary (occasional sightings of the greylag goose here), Palheiro Ferreiro golf course (swifts, grey herons, rock doves, etc.), and the coastline between Funchal and Cabo Girão (kestrels, buzzards and lesser black-backed gulls). Ruddy turnstones and the occasional sparrowhawk have also been seen around **Funchal harbour**. Near the water's edge, keep an eye out for the oystercatcher, the little egret, and periodic visitors like the grey wagtail (actually grey and yellow). Two bird species are endemic to Madeira: the long-toed pigeon (*Columba trocaz*) and the Freira – the laurel forest is their natural habitat. The canary – indigenous to Macronesia – is commonplace while Berthelot's pipit, a small warbler with greyish-brown, almost tawny feathers, has been spotted in numbers around Ponta de São Lourenço. Also look out for endemic subspecies, including the yellow-legged gull, the blackcap (a small warbler attracted to shrubs, even in the gardens of Funchal), the firecrest (another warbler with a distinctive red and gold head stripe, preferring a

> **USEFUL WEBSITES**
>
> • Search engine for sites on Madeira: **www.madeira online.com** – still useful even though some of the information is out of date.
> • Official tourist board site: **www.madeiratourism.org**
> • Madeira Explores, specialists in walking tours: **www. madeira-levada-walks.com**
> • Company specializing in mountain bike hire, canyoning, jeep safari, jet ski rental, trekking, etc.: **www.madeira- island.com/aventura**
> • Books, cakes, wine, CDs, etc.: **www.madeira- shopping.com**

Opposite: *Distinctive A-frame houses are typical of the Santana region.*
Below: *Strelitizias and proteas thrive in the semitropical Madeira climate.*

> **DAYS OF THE WEEK**
>
> If you're looking to check the opening and closing times of a restaurant, bar, theatre, etc., it might help to know the days of the week in Portuguese, which differ from the French, Italian or Spanish pattern. They are:
> **Domingo:** Sunday
> **Segunda-feira:** Monday
> **Terça-feira:** Tuesday
> **Quarta-feira:** Wednesday
> **Quinta-feira:** Thursday
> **Sexta-feira:** Friday
> **Sábado:** Saturday

Below: *Typical Madeiran landscape – nearly half the island lies above 700m (2297ft).*

woodland habitat), and the chaffinch. Porto Santo is the breeding ground of the hoopoe. Its highly distinctive colouring (fawn, with startling black and white bars on wings and tail) makes it easy to identify. If you're looking for a memento of your visit, ask about the stamp series *Madeiran Birds*, issued by the Portuguese post office.

Climate

Madeira is renowned for its mild, **subtropical** climate: average annual temperatures of around 22°C (72°F) in summer, usually falling no lower than 16°C (61°F) in winter. The Gulf Stream ensures that sea temperatures too are invitingly warm, ranging from a low of 17°C (63°F) in March to a high of 23°C (73°F) in September. What complicates the picture is the effect of microclimates on weather patterns. As any regular visitor will confirm, the Paúl da Serra may be shrouded in freezing mist, while Funchal basks in warm sunshine. Generally speaking, the south coast is the hottest part of the island, particularly the Bay of Funchal that is sheltered by a ridge of

mountains to the rear. On the sunniest days, the temperature can climb to 27°C (81°F) or even higher. The humidity too is more tolerable here, thanks to cooling onshore breezes. Nevertheless, the capital is not immune to the effects of the *capacete* (peaked cap or helmet), a bank of cloud which blankets the coast from late morning to mid-afternoon when it

Above: *Tropical fruits make a colourful display in a Funchal market.*

retreats to the mountains. This phenomenon (irritating to sunbathers) is most pronounced in February, March and June. If you're looking for uninterrupted sunshine, your best bet is **Porto Santo**. Much less bearable than the *capacete* is the *leste*, a searing easterly originating in the North African desert which can send temperatures rocketing to 40°C (104°F) for a few days each summer, when humidity levels sink to 13% or even lower. At this time the air fills with a fine, reddish Saharan dust. By contrast, the average temperature on the north coast is around 1.5°C lower than the south, while humidity is up to 10% higher. Further inland, the mountainous areas are cloudy for much of the year, to an altitude of around 1200m (3937ft). Above that level, however, visibility is usually excellent.

Many visitors to Madeira are surprised by the amount of **rainfall**. Generally speaking, windy, rainy days are more frequently encountered on the exposed northern coast than in the south. For example, while precipitation in Funchal averages 550mm (22 inches) per annum, it is nearly four times higher in

FUNCHAL	J	F	M	A	M	J	J	A	S	O	N	D
MIN TEMP. °C	13	13	13	14	16	17	19	19	19	18	16	14
MAX TEMP. °C	19	18	19	19	21	22	24	24	24	23	22	19
MIN TEMP. °F	56	56	56	58	60	63	66	67	67	65	61	58
MAX TEMP. °F	66	65	66	67	69	72	75	76	76	74	71	67
RAINFALL mm	64	74	79	33	18	5	0	0	25	76	89	84
RAINFALL in.	2.5	2.9	3.1	1.3	0.7	0.2	0.0	0.0	1.0	3.0	3.5	3.3
DAYS OF RAINFALL	6.0	6.0	7.0	4.0	2.0	0.9	0.2	0.4	3.0	7.0	6.0	7.0

Fruits in Season

Custard apples: January–April
Strawberries: March–June
Cherries, apricots: May, June
Pawpaw, figs: June–October
Plums: June, July
Grapes, melons: August–October
Mangoes, avocados: September–December
Grapefruit: September–November.
Pears, apples: October–March
Oranges: November–March
Bananas: year-round

The Real Columbus?

During the 1980s an entertaining, if far-fetched thesis was put forward that the discoverer of America was not an Italian born in Genoa in 1451 but a Portuguese, born in the Alentejo three years earlier. Even more sensational was the claim that Christopher Columbus was really Salvador Fernandes Zarco, illegitimate son of the Duke of Beja, grandson of the discoverer of Madeira, João Gonçalves Zarco, and great-nephew of Henry the Navigator. The story goes that he adopted the name Columbus in 1485 on the orders of King João II – part of his cover as a member of the Portuguese secret service. His task? To convince the King and Queen of the viability of a *western* sea route to the Indies, leaving the Portuguese navigators, Bartholomeu Dias and Vasco da Gama, to open up the eastern route via the Cape of Good Hope!

the north, thanks to cyclonic Atlantic fronts which deposit the rainfall on the slopes of the forested hinterland. Even in the capital, however, some rain can be expected from October to May, usually in the form of short but violent cloudbursts. Again, Porto Santo is the ideal refuge for anyone averse to rainfall.

Levadas

Unlike the Canary Islands or Porto Santo, Madeira is blessed with a super-abundant **water supply**. One scientist has estimated that the hidden reserves amount to a staggering 8 billion cubic metres, enough to last not only the present millenium but many more to come. The problem is that while the south of the island enjoys most of the sunshine and is potentially more fertile, most of the rainfall is concentrated in the north. The early Portuguese settlers wasted little time in coming up with a solution – a system of narrow watercourses channelling rain and spring water directly to the fruit orchards and sugar plantations along the south coast. Today these *levadas* (from the Portuguese *levar*, 'to carry') crisscross the island, covering a distance of more than 2150km (1335 miles). No mean feat, when you consider that the labourers used only chisels and pick-axes and risked life and limb cutting their way into the sheer rock, sometimes suspended in hanging baskets over steep precipices, or crawling on their hands and knees through tunnels hewn in the mountainside.

The *levadas* are administered directly by the Madeiran government, which charges farmers and market gardeners for the service by the 'flow hour'. Day-to-day management is in the hands of the *levadeiro* who is responsible for operating the sluice gates (water is channelled to the farms following a pre-arranged timetable), for repairing fire or storm damage and for clearing away leaves and other debris. Pathways, designed originally for the convenience of the *levadeiro*, have become an important source of income for the island's burgeoning tourist industry, as visitors come to realize that **levada walking** is one of the more exhilarating ways of appreciating the diversity of Madeira's landscape.

HISTORY IN BRIEF

According to the Portuguese chronicler, Gomes de Azurara, the Madeiran archipelago was discovered by chance. In 1418 two naval commanders, **João Gonçalves Zarco** and **Tristão Vaz Teixeira**, were exploring the west coast of Africa when they were blown off course during a storm and washed ashore on Porto Santo. When they returned to Sagres, their base in the Algarve, they reported having seen a much larger island to the south, shrouded in mist. The Portuguese heir to the throne, the Infante Enrique (better known as Henry the Navigator), ordered them back to investigate and, in 1420, they found their mystery island which Zarco christened Madeira, '**the wooded isle**'. In fact, the discovery of Madeira is unlikely to have been an accident. All the islands in the archipelago had been charted by the end of the 14th century and the Medici Atlas, compiled by Genoese cartographers in 1351, even refers to Madeira as the 'wooded island' (Isola de Lolegname in Italian dialect). It seems unlikely then that Henry the Navigator, the founder of a School of Seamanship, would have been unaware of their existence. In any event, Madeira and Porto Santo were officially declared Portuguese territory in 1425 and handed over to Henry's captains to administer.

ROMAN MADEIRA

Most experts now agree that the existence of Madeira was known long before Zarco stumbled on the island in 1418. It may be that the archipelago was familiar even to the Romans. In his *Natural History*, written in or around AD77, Pliny the Younger mentions the 'Purple Islands', referring to the dyes extracted from the sap of dragon trees on Porto Santo (actually reddish in colour). Pliny also knew of the Canaries, which he christened the 'Fortunate Isles'. Not long after Pliny, the cartographer Ptolemy used the archipelago as his marker for zero-degree longtitude.

Below: *Traditional* azulejos *(painted tiles) add to the appeal of the Monte Palace Tropical Garden.*

MALMSEY

In England, **Malvasia wine** is also known as Malmsey. In 1478, the nobleman George Duke of Clarence was dispatched to the Tower of London on a charge of high treason. Told to prepare for death, he was invited (so it is said) to choose a means of execution and asked to be drowned in a butt (vat) of Malmsey. In Shakespeare's *Richard III*, the duke is stabbed first: 'Take that, and that; if all this will not do, I'll drown you in the malmsey-butt within'. According to the bard, Malmsey was also the favourite tipple of Sir John Falstaff (*see Henry IV Part 2*).

João Gonçalves, nicknamed Zarco ('one-eyed') after losing an eye at the Siege of Ceuta (Morocco), was assigned the west of the island and governed from Funchal, while his companion, Teixeira, took charge of the east from his base at Machico. The Italian adventurer, Bartolomeu Perestrelo, who had joined them on their second voyage, oversaw the settlement of Porto Santo. The arrangement seems to have worked well.

The Early Settlers

Colonization began almost immediately. First on the scene were the scions of the **Portuguese nobility** who formed the island's landowning elite. Their names – Freitas, Bettencourt, Almeida, etc. – live on to this day through their innumerable descendants. There were also distinguished exiles: Sir John Drummond, a refugee from the Scottish court, for example, and a former king of Poland, known locally as Enrique Alemão. More crucial to the development of the island's economy were the entrepreneurs and merchant-financiers from Italy, Spain and northern Europe (especially the Flemish ports of Bruges and Antwerp). Artisans and labourers from mainland Portugal provided the workforce until the first contingent of slaves arrived from the Canary Islands in 1452.

For Zarco, clearing the dense virgin forest for cultivation was a priority. Great swathes were set alight and left to burn out of control for weeks, even months on end – seven years, according to one chronicler! Today's environmentalists would not have approved of the wholesale destruction, but the tree ash did add to the fertility of the volcanic soil. To stimulate agriculture, the

CRISTOVÃO COLOMBO

HISTORY IN BRIEF

Historical Calendar

20mBC Madeira is formed from spectacular volcanic eruptions beneath the surface of the Atlantic Ocean.
1.7mBC As the volcanoes cool, a distinctive Madeiran landscape begins to take shape.
AD77 There is a reference to Madeira in Pliny the Younger's *Natural History*.
1351 A Genoese map identifies three islands off the African coast. Madeira is named the 'Wooded Isle' (Isola de Lolegname).
1418 The naval commanders, João Gonçalves Zarco and Tristão Vaz Teixeira, step ashore on Porto Santo for the first time.
1419–20 The Portuguese colonization of Porto Santo and Madeira begins with the blessing of Prince Henry the Navigator.
1425 Madeira is officially declared a province of Portugal.
1452 The first slaves arrive on Madeira from the Canary Islands. They work the sugar plantations and begin building a network of irrigation channels (*levadas*).
1478 The explorer, Christopher Columbus, then a sugar merchant, visits Funchal on business, before marrying the daughter of the governor of Porto Santo.
1514 According to the island's first census, the population is 5000, excluding slaves.
1566 The French adventurer, Bernard de Montluc, sacks Funchal and massacres the garrison (250 men).
1580–1640 Madeira is ruled from Spain after Philip II claims the Portuguese crown.
1662 The marriage of Charles II of England to Catherine of Braganza, daughter of João IV of Portugal, boosts trade with Madeira.
1703 The Methuen Treaty further encourages British merchants to settle on Madeira. Soon the wine trade is almost exclusively in their hands.
1768 The British navigator and explorer, Captain Cook, calls at Madeira on his first voyage in the *Endeavour*.
1801–02 First British occupation of the island during the Napoleonic Wars.
1807–14 Second British occupation. Many of the 2000 garrison choose to stay on and settle.
1846 Potato crop fails.
1851 The fungus *Oidium tuckeri* attacks the vines, devastating the crop.
1856 A cholera epidemic kills around 10,000 inhabitants.
1891 Reid's Hotel opens, stimulating tourism.
1916 Germany declares war on Portugal and Funchal is shelled by U-boats.
1931 A general strike is declared on Madeira following a banking collapse and a sudden rise in bread prices. An attempted coup d'état is put down by the Portuguese army.
1939–45 World War II. Portugal remains neutral, but Reid's Hotel closes and refugees from Gibraltar take shelter on the island.
1964 The opening of Santa Catarina airport ends the long isolation of the island.
1974 Democracy is restored in Portugal after a bloodless military coup.
1976 Madeira is granted special status as an autonomous region within Portugal.
1986 Portugal enters the EU, bringing increased investment to the island.
1997 Via Rápida motorway opens on the south coast.
2002 The redevelopment and expansion of Funchal airport is completed.
2004 Madeira is chosen as the European Union Region of the Year.
2007 Madeira enters Guinness Book of Records for staging world's largest fireworks display.

fields and clearings were leased to members of the aristocracy for a specified period, during which they were expected to make improvements on the land that would eventually be theirs. This incentive scheme seems to have paid off. Grain and other cereals were grown for subsistence, while the first vine terraces were planted on the

Opposite: *Christopher Columbus married a daughter of Bartolomeu Perestrelo, one of the founders of Madeira.*

Above: *Madeira has been producing quality wines since the 16th century.*
Opposite: *This shrine to the Virgin Mary at Terreiro da Luta was erected in the 1920s.*

hillsides of the southern coast. The extremely lucrative trade in **sugar** ('white gold') began in the 1470s and peaked in 1506. Christopher Columbus was just one of a galaxy of **foreign merchants** who profited from the export of this precious commodity to markets across Europe. These entrepreneurs dominated banking, commerce and shipping on the island and had a controlling interest in the timber yards. Conducting their business outside the Customs House in Funchal, they were immediately recognizable by their fashionable dress and ostentatious behaviour. Some married into the Portuguese nobility, while many bought land and eventually settled down on the island – men like Giovanni Lomelino, whose descendants built Quinta das Cruzes; Simone Acciaiuoli, a noted collector of Flemish art; and Jennin d'Esmerandt, one of Madeira's most powerful plantation owners and a friend of Columbus. By 1508, Funchal had a population in excess of 5000 and was Portugal's third city after Lisbon and Porto. It owed much of its prosperity to the **slave workforce**, which now numbered around 3000: Guanches from the Canary Islands worked alongside Berbers from North Africa, Guineans and men and women from the Portuguese East Indies. It was these human chattels who built the sugar mills, laboured on the plantations and constructed the first *levadas*.

From Sugar to Wine

Sometime the bubble had to burst. Over-production, soil exhaustion, the increasing cost of slaves and, most importantly, competition from Brazil slowly eroded Madeira's lead in the sugar trade. Demand began falling in the first decade of the 16th century, but the islanders were quick

---

SLAVES AND SUGAR

Portuguese historians have recently challenged the commonly held assumption that Madeira's sugar plantations were worked exclusively by slaves. Records for the parish of Calheta (a major sugar-producing area) show that just 7% of the island's slaves were resident there. In fact the highest concentration of slaves was in Funchal, not a major sugar-producing area. Labour on the plantations was mixed, free men working alongside slaves for wages or payment in kind. The Madeiran sugar industry could have survived without any slave involvement at all.

to find an alternative source of revenue. Within 50 years most of the plantations had become vineyards. The nascent industry flourished thanks largely to the introduction of the **Malvasia grape** from the Greek islands – visitors to Madeira, like the Venetian navigator Alvise de Mosto, commented on the quality of the wine being produced. Among the more innovative cultivators were the Jesuits, who opened a college on the island in 1572. The quality of the Malvasia from their vineyards at Quinta Grande (west of Cabo Girão) and Fajã dos Padres was legendary and they are usually credited with introducing new varieties like Bual and Sercial. While the Spanish occupation of Portugal from 1580–1640 had a negative impact on sales – the Spanish were keen to promote their own wines – by the mid-17th century, Madeira was exporting 12,000 barrels annually, to the American colonies, the West Indies and Europe.

For the islanders, the only fly in the ointment was the very real threat of **pirate attack**. Porto Santo was particularly vulnerable to raids by corsairs from the Barbary Coast. In 1617 Algerian sailors wreaked havoc on the population, massacring most of the men and taking the women and children captive. The psychological scars remained with the survivors, who left Porto Santo for good, taking refuge in the hills of Santo da Serra. On the mainland the worst incident took place in 1566 when a French adventurer, Bertrand de Montluc, attacked Funchal, wiping out the garrison before unleashing his force of 1000 men on the beleaguered inhabitants.

MADEIRA – THE US CONNECTION

From 1668 only Madeiran wines were allowed into Britain's American colonies and within 50 years the American market accounted for around 25% of total sales. A genuine liking for Madeira soon developed, so much so that in 1768 a riot broke out in Boston Harbour when British customs officials tried to impound a consignment of smuggled wine – a dress rehearsal for the famous tea party five years later. Madeira was used to toast the Declaration of Independence in 1776 and to mark the inauguration of George Washington as first US president in 1789. The drink remained fashionable throughout the 19th century but never recovered from the impact of Prohibition. There are still aficionados in Georgia, however, where the Madeira Club of Savannah holds regular meetings.

The British Connection

England and Portugal sealed what was to become the longest political association in history in 1386, when King João I married Philippa of Lancaster, the future mother of Henry the Navigator.

POISON PEN

One visitor's impressions were not published in her lifetime. The Englishwoman Isabella de França spent her honeymoon on Madeira in 1853 – her husband was the son of a local merchant. The newlyweds, aged 58 and 50 respectively, threw themselves into the social round, Isabella later confiding her frequently acerbic thoughts to her diary, which she illustrated herself. *Journal of a Visit to Madeira and Portugal* was finally published in 1969. The original forms part of the collection of the **Casa Museu Frederico de Freitas** in Funchal. (It was Dr Freitas who discovered the manuscript in the 1930s, gathering dust in a local bookshop.)

British interest in Madeira, however, was slower to develop. Trading concessions granted by King João IV in 1654 were renewed following the marriage between Charles II of England and the Portuguese princess, Catherine of Braganza, in 1662. Shortly afterwards Madeira was exempted from protectionist measures aimed at boosting British exports at the expense of the Dutch, their long-standing rivals on the high seas. This gave Madeira's British merchants a virtual trading monopoly with the American colonies as well as the West Indies. Their business interests were further consolidated by the Methuen Treaty of 1703 which dramatically reduced the import duty paid on Madeiran wines entering England.

While the merchants lived lives of unashamed luxury on their *quintas* and vineyards, ordinary Madeirans fared less well. Effectively the island's economy had been transformed into a **monoculture** dependent on wine (up to 70% of cereals were now imported). Crop failures, a fall in wine prices, or a dramatic shift in the political climate (the American War of Independence, for example) were harbingers of famine and destitution for the poorest sections of the population. Unemployment, low wages and other social ills were laid at the door of the British, who were often perceived as arrogant or condescending. The precarious nature of the Madeiran economy was even more keenly felt as the population continued to rise, from around 50,000 in 1754 to 84,000 half a century later.

Opposite: *A decorative feature in the tropical gardens of Quinta das Cruzes, Funchal.*
Right: *An old town scene on azulejos.*

When British interests in Madeira were threatened during the Napoleonic Wars, the immediate response was to occupy the island – not once, but twice (1801–02 and 1807–14). A rash of intermarriages (not to mention less formal sexual liaisons) was one consequence, and when the garrison finally disbanded, many soldiers chose to stay on, among them the future wine merchant John Blandy. Madeira was to witness the final act of the Napoleonic era when, in August 1815, *HMS Northumberland*, en route to St Helena with the banished former emperor on board, dropped anchor in Funchal harbour. The British consul, **Henry Veitch**, visited the ship and provoked a minor diplomatic incident by addressing Bonaparte as his majesty, a faux pas which eventually led to his dismissal.

The Birth of Tourism

Just off the Avenida do Infante in Funchal, visitors can still see the beautiful grounds of the **Hospício da Princesa**. The hospice for sufferers of tuberculosis was founded by the Empress of Brazil in memory of her daughter, Maria Amélia, who died of the disease in 1853 at the age of 22. The unfortunate young woman was one of thousands of invalids who came to Madeira hoping that its famously mild winter climate, recommended by doctors throughout Europe, would improve their health. By the end of the 19th century there were even guidebooks written specifically for patients, for example the Marquis degli Albizzi's *Madère: Guide practique pour malades et touristes*. Travelling with the invalids were their physicians, nurses

FOREIGN AID

The economic crisis of the 1840s and 1850s was so grave that the governor of Madeira twice appealed to the international community for relief. The contributing countries included Great Britain, the United States, Germany, Russia and Ireland – this at the time of the potato famine. On a visit to Madeira in 1849 the Dean of Ely commented that 'not even in the worst parts of Ireland' had he seen 'more intense misery than among the people of this island'.

Right: *Fish hanging out to dry on the waterfront of Câmara de Lobos.*
Opposite: *Madeira's recently modernized international airport is only a short drive from Funchal.*

NAPOLEON'S MADEIRA

During his famous stay in 1950, Sir Winston Churchill gave a dinner for the British community in Reid's Hotel. As a special treat he served his guests bottles of 1792 vintage Madeira, regaling them with the story of how the British consul, Henry Veitch, presented Napoleon with a consignment of this finely aged wine on his way to exile in 1815. This intriguing anecdote seems to have originated with one of Madeira's great characters, Dr Michael Grabham, who owned the wine in the 1930s. Cold water has since been poured on the story by Alex Liddell in his book *Madeira* (Faber, 1998). Liddell points out that, as this particular wine was not bottled until 1840, it could hardly have been offered to Napoleon, who died 20 years earlier. According to Grabham's son, Walter, Grabham senior had a tendency to 'embroider some of his statements.'

and companions who whiled away the time writing letters, keeping diaries, sketching, painting or compiling travelogues. Some of their output (mainly engravings and watercolours of the exotic flora, fauna and scenery) is exhibited in the **Quinta das Cruzes Museum** and offers a fascinating insight into the early travellers' perception of the island. When they returned home, the more colourful accounts appeared in magazines like the *Illustrated London News*, fanning interest. While the voyage from Liverpool to Funchal still took around 13 days, the number of visitors was increasing at a remarkable rate, so much so that by the middle of the 19th century Madeira's income from tourism was estimated at around £40,000 a year. Not only the sick, but colonial civil servants on leave from India and the Far East, clergymen, vacationing businessmen and their spouses, journalists, artists, botanists and geologists all found much to wonder at. Visiting royalty brought an extra cachet to the island. Following Prince Adalbert of Prussia came Queen Adelaide (widow of William IV of England), Princess Maria Carlotta of Saxony, Archduke Maximilian von Habsburg and the Empress Elisabeth of Austria. For the British, who formed by far the largest contingent, Funchal soon became a home-from-home with its English church, croquet lawns, tea gardens, cricket and football matches, not to mention Consul Veitch's notorious 'Madeira parties'. Also *de rigueur* was to sit for a portrait at Senhor Vicente's photographic studio, which opened in 1865 to cater for the growing demand for holiday souvenirs.

Hard Times

Few contemporary travelogues make mention of the series of **disasters** of near Biblical proportions which visited the island around mid-century. First, in 1846, the potato crop failed. Then, in 1851, a fungus, *Oidium tuckeri*, began attacking the vines with such devastating effect that many experts wrote off the industry altogether. While the islanders were still reeling under these blows, cholera struck, killing around 10,000 men, women and children – 10% of the population. Finally, the vine louse, *Phylloxera*, decimated the wine harvests of 1872–82. Thousands of agricultural workers were reduced to begging on the streets as the government launched not one, but a succession of appeals for international aid. For many, however, the response was too little too late, leaving **emigration** as the only way out. By 1910 more than 80,000 men, women and children had vacated the island for good, creating a Madeiran **diaspora** in Brazil, Guyana, Angola and South Africa. They are remembered today in the Monument to the Madeiran Emigrant on Funchal's waterfront.

> **JUMPING FLEA**
>
> The *braguinha* (see page 27) takes its name from the northern Portuguese town of Braga where it was originally known as the *cavaquinho*. Madeiran emigrants hoping to start a new life in Hawaii towards the end of the 19th century brought the unusual four-stringed instrument with them. It was an immediate hit with the Pacific islanders, who were so impressed by the performers' deftness of touch that they re-christened the *braguinha* 'jumping flea' (**ukulele**). One of the more enterprising Madeiran families – Nunes by name – began marketing a more compact version of the instrument that was patented in the United States in 1917. The ukulele's heyday was the 1920s when it featured in numerous minstrel shows and Vaudeville turns.

The Twentieth Century

The new century began with a crisis of a different kind. In 1905, the German government approached the Portuguese with proposals for an ambitious development programme for the island. On reading the small print, Lisbon discovered that the plans included not only the building of new hospitals and sanatoria as originally promised, but a string of luxury hotels and even a casino (gambling was illegal at that time). The British suspected (not without reason) that what was actually envisaged

> **SELVAGENS**
>
> No book on Madeira would be complete without at least a mention of this remote Madeiran dependency, more than 280km (174 miles) south of Funchal (closer in fact to the Canaries). The name means 'wild' or 'savage' and applies to a tiny cluster of reefs and islets declared a **nature reserve** in 1971. Completely uninhabited, the Selvagens are visited mainly by shearwaters, grebes, petrels and other **seabirds**, and are the preserve of rare **flora** – 10 of the 90 plant species found here are endemic. The Selvagens currently form part of a study into the volcanic origins of the archipelago by European geophysicists. On a more romantic note, rumours persist that this is where the notorious Scottish pirate, Captain Kidd, buried his treasure before he was captured and executed in 1701. So far, however, not a single doubloon has been recovered.

was a commercial takeover of the island, and persuaded the Portuguese to renege on the agreement. Relations between the Germans and the Portuguese soured as a consequence, and deteriorated further when German property on Madeira was confiscated at the outbreak of World War I. In December 1916 Funchal was lightly shelled following a U-boat attack on Allied shipping but, apart from a similar incident the following year, the island emerged from the conflict relatively unscathed. The damage to the economy (both wine exports and tourism), however, was considerable.

In the postwar period, Portugal's political instability mirrored the situation elsewhere in Europe. A military coup in 1924 brought a hitherto obscure economics professor, **Dr Antonio Salazar**, to prominence. By 1933 Salazar was effectively a dictator, retaining power until his death in 1968. The consequences for Madeira were felt even before Salazar was securely in the saddle. In 1931 his stringent financial policy led to a sudden hike in bread prices and a banking collapse which, at a stroke, wiped out many of the islanders' savings. A general strike was declared, supported by several hundred recently exiled political prisoners. Lisbon despatched troops to quell the unrest but some of them defected, leading to an attempted coup by rebel general Sousa Dias. The Portuguese eventually put down the uprising but not before panic set in among the British residents, many of whom fled the island.

Right: *Madeira is a dependency of Portugal.*

Economically speaking, Madeira remained the poor relation throughout the Salazar dictatorship until his successor was overthrown in a bloodless coup, known as the 'Carnation Revolution', in 1974. The restoration of **democracy** was followed two years later by the introduction of a new constitution, which gave Madeira a greater degree of autonomy than it had ever previously enjoyed. For an entertaining overview of Madeiran history, visit the Madeira Story Centre (see page 51).

GOVERNMENT AND ECONOMY

The Portuguese constitution of 1976 designates the Madeiran archipelago an Autonomous Political Region. The people of the island elect a head of state, the President, along with the 50 members of the parliament or Legislative Assembly. This body is responsible for all matters of direct concern to the island, including taxation, customs duties and public services. Madeirans also elect five deputies to the Portuguese parliament. The government in Lisbon oversees foreign policy and defence, and has the final say in all constitutional issues. Portugal's representative on the island, the Minister of the Republic, has a residence in Funchal. The Madeiran President appoints a cabinet comprising a vice president and six secretaries of state. Local government is in the hands of elected town councils.

For more than a quarter of a century, power has been in the hands of the conservative **Popular Social Democratic Party** (PSD), which won the first elections (1976) by a landslide, with around 65% of the vote. Their leader, the charismatic Dr Alberto João Jardim, became president in 1978 and is still in office.

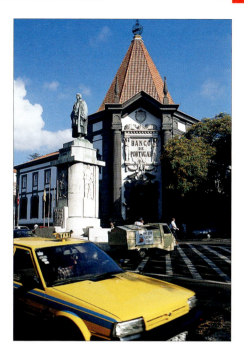

Above: *A monument to João Gonçalves Zarco by the island's most famous artist, Francisco Franco. It was unveiled in 1934 and won the praise of the Portuguese dictator, Dr Salazar.*

Right: *Bananas account for nearly half the island's total exports.*
Opposite: *Fishermen play cards to while away the idle hours.*

Madeira and the European Union

The mainstays of the Madeiran economy are farming, viticulture, fishing, handicrafts (mainly embroidery and wickerwork), tourism, and offshore financial services. Agriculture still employs more than one fifth (21%) of the workforce. The most important single crop is bananas, accounting for 45% of the island's total exports. **Tourism** is an increasingly visible source of revenue, the majority of visitors coming from Portugal, Britain and Western Europe, including Scandinavia. While unemployment has fallen to around 4% (a much lower figure than on the mainland), the Madeiran GDP per capita is only 30% of the European average and less than 60% of the average Portuguese.

Impressive levels of economic growth have been achieved (albeit from a very low base) since Portugal joined the European Union in 1986. Two decades of political stability have undoubtedly helped, but the unprecedented rise in the living standards of most Madeirans during the 1990s would have been inconceivable without massive EU funding. During 1990–93 alone, the Community contributed US$370m to developing the island's infrastructure, and by 2005 the Regional Development Fund and other European agencies were

---

MADEIRA INTERNATIONAL AIRPORT

The redevelopment of Funchal's international airport, 16km (10 miles) east of Funchal, described as the 'project of the (20th) century', was finally completed in 2002. The centrepiece is the extended runway, now 2781m (9124ft), facilitating the arrival of wide-bodied intercontinental aircraft such as the Airbus A340 and Boeing 747-400. Other improvements include the enlarged and completely refurbished terminal, with more than double the number of check-in counters. The airport has a handling capacity of 3.5 million passengers a year. It was formerly known as Santa Caterina airport.

providing close on 80% of total investment. To date, most of the money has been spent on road construction, schools, hospitals and vocational training. The most ambitious single project, the redevelopment of Funchal airport, cost upwards of €355m. According to the then Madeiran vice-president, João Cunha e Silva, it was the islands' 'appropriate and effective application of Community funds' which led the European Union to designate them **European Region of the Year** for 2004. In a canny move, the government persuaded the Portuguese International and Manchester United footballer, Cristiano Ronaldo (a native of Madeira), to be its public face at European Trade Fairs.

HERITAGE

One of the most active Madeiran communities abroad hails from **New Bedford** on the eastern seaboard of the United States. It was towards the end of the 18th century that American whalers began calling at **Caniçal** to enlist experienced crews for expeditions out in the Atlantic. More often than not, the final destination was New Bedford, where many Madeiran sailors eventually chose to settle. The Club Madeirense SS Sacramento is dedicated to preserving Madeiran customs and traditions and, with the active support of President Jardim, has recently financed the Museum of Madeiran Heritage. New Bedford also has its own home-grown folk band, the Grupo Folkloric Madeirense.

THE PEOPLE

The majority of Madeirans are of Portuguese origin, descendants of settlers from the Algarve and Alentejo who began colonizing the island in the 15th century. **Portuguese** is the official language and mother tongue of Madeirans, though English is spoken by a growing number of young people and is widely used in business. The population figure of 241,000 does not include the diaspora of around one million expatriate Madeirans, living in countries as far apart as Venezuela and South Africa. Emigration has been a significant demographic factor since the middle of the 19th century, though the trend has recently been reversed. Not all the returning migrant families are welcomed with open arms. While they bring investment and entrepreneurial skills, their relative prosperity and extravagant lifestyle are the underlying causes of resentment.

Madeira still remains a deeply **conservative** society committed to the traditional values of home

Sisi

One of the most famous 19th-century celebrities to visit Madeira was the Empress Elisabeth (Sisi) of Austria. Her marriage to Franz Josef I was an unhappy one and, as time went on, the popular, much-fêted empress spent more and more time away from home. She spent the winter of 1861–62 on Madeira amid rumours that she was suffering from tuberculosis – on the evidence, a venereal infection caught from her husband seems more likely. Sisi died tragically in October 1898, stabbed to death by an Italian anarchist while vacationing on the shores of Lake Geneva.

and family. The **Roman Catholic Church**, which claims the allegiance of around 97% of the population, exercises a powerful influence in this respect. However, there are growing signs of change as a younger generation, increasingly educated outside the island and finding work in the towns rather than the countryside, questions the old mode of thinking.

The Traditional Way of Life

To discover how Madeirans observe their time-honoured customs and traditions, check out a typical village **festival** *(festa)*. These lively celebrations usually mark the feast day of the local saint or one of the red-letter days in the agricultural calendar (the grape or chestnut harvest, for example). Some festivals are associated with a local legend or miraculous event – the crucifix recovered from the sea near Machico, for instance. The procession to the church of Our Lady of Monte which takes place on the Feast of the Assumption (15 August) is the most solemn of these occasions and attracts pilgrims from all over the island.

Folk music is another Madeiran tradition worth investigating, though nowadays it is the exclusive preserve of bands and choirs, performing in hotels or established venues like the Café Relógio in Camacha. Well-known names who have recorded on CD include the Grupo Folclórico da Camacha, Banda d'Alem and Encontros da Eira. Songs like *Cerfeiras* (The Harvesters) and *Baile do paspalhao* (Dance of the Lark) relate to life in the fields. *Na Noite do pão* (Night of the Bread) was traditionally sung on Christmas Eve by women baking bread for the following day's festivities. Crafts too had their own tunes, the embroiderers' *Si Que Brade*, for example. Songs of Moorish origin include the *Cantiga do preto* (Black Man's Song), characterized by a monotonous drum beat, and the *Carrier's Dance*, in which the performers imitate the ponderous movements of men and women carrying heavy loads, their feet

Above: *Plaintive strains of* fado *music emanate from the restaurants of Funchal's Old Quarter.*
Opposite: *Folk troupes perform for tourists during major festivals.*

weighed down by chains. In a lighter vein, the **dance** of the *Camacheiras* features a young couple who stop to argue on the way to a feast, until they're enveloped by other merrymakers and their quarrel is forgotten. All dancers wear the standard Madeiran **folk costume** of white shirts and baggy trousers (men) or white blouse with red embroidered cape and waistcoat and long, multi-coloured striped skirt (women). Men and women wear the *carapuca*, a skullcap with a twirled point. They perform to the accompaniment of the *rajão* or *braguinha* (both relatives of the mandolin), the *raspadeiro* (a notched stick played like a washboard), *castanholes* (castanets) and the *briquinho*, rings of cloth puppets which dance and jangle as the stick to which they are attached is pounded on the ground.

Embroidery

The art of embroidery (***bordados***) arrived on Madeira with the discoverers – in those days it was more or less the exclusive preserve of Portuguese noblewomen. Some of the oldest surviving examples, created by the nuns of the Santa Clara Convent in Funchal, are now on display in the Museu de Arte Sacra. The cottage industry that brought the beauty and complexity of Madeiran embroidery to the notice of the world is of more recent origin and was the

FADO

Fado (the word means 'fate') is to the Portuguese what Flamenco is to the Spanish. Plaintive and dramatic, the songs (usually ballads) tell of lost or unrequited love and the vicissitudes of life: 'soul' music, one might say. *Fado* is said to have originated in the drinking dens of Lisbon, and may have African or Arab roots. Accompaniment is usually provided by the guitar. The best place to hear authentic *fado* (if a little touristy) is Arsénio's in Funchal's old town.

Above: *Colourful Madeiran hats for sale.*

WICKERWORK

Wickerwork (*Vimes*) is the most important Madeiran handicraft after embroidery. A British sugar merchant, William Hinton, saw the commercial possibilities in the 1850s when he began supplying local hotels with the then fashionable cane furniture. **Camacha**, the village where Hinton owned a summer home, is still the weaving 'capital' of the island. Today wickerwork employs around 2500 people and is an important source of livelihood for the farmers around **Boaventura**, where most of the willow plantations are concentrated.

initiative of an Englishwoman, Elizabeth Phelps. The daughter of a highly respected wine merchant and philanthropist, she taught needlework at an orphanage in Santana. Her fascination with traditional Madeiran embroidery led her to take samples to England, where they caused a minor sensation at the Great Exhibition of 1851 in London. Almost overnight Madeiran embroidery came into vogue, especially for wedding gowns – so much so that demand outstripped supply until a British firm set the business on a more commercial footing in 1862. More than 1000 jobs were created, an unexpected boon for the many women whose husbands were out of work following the crisis in the vineyards. When the fashion eventually ran its course around 1900, a German entrepreneur, Otto von Streit, came to the rescue with the labour-saving technique of printing the designs directly onto the fabric. This revolutionized the business and by the 1920s, around 70,000 women were employed in the craft. Today the figure is closer to 10,000, but embroidery still outstrips wine in terms of exports.

The seamstresses, known as *bordadeiras*, work from home, their skills passed within families from one generation to the next. The materials – cotton, linen, natural silk and organdie – and the patterns are supplied by agents working on a commission basis. Usually two or three women work on one item, each specializing in a particular stitch or design embellishment. The finishing touches are added at the 'factory' where the embroideries are washed and ironed before receiving the official seal of authenticity from IBTAM (see page 51). Italy, Germany, France and the United Kingdom are the most important export markets. Despite a good showing at the Lisbon World Exhibition in 1998, Madeiran embroiderers have found it increasingly difficult to compete with China and the Far East, where labour costs are lower and marketing more aggressive.

Food

Madeiran cooking differs little from that of mainland Portugal; however, there are one or two pleasant surprises in the way of regional specialities – the scabbard fish (**espada**) for example. No one visiting the fish market in Funchal will forget the serrated teeth and repellent, almost insolent stare of this creature of the deep. But the white flesh is both tender and succulent and goes down a treat with the traditional side dish of bananas fried in butter. Parrot fish (bodião), tuna (atum), sea bream (pargo), hake (pescada) and mackerel (carapau) are the supporting cast. Bacalhau (salted cod, shredded and fried with onions, egg, garlic and potatoes) and cataplana (a seafood casserole of clams, prawns, squid and white fish, cooked with herbs and accompanied by a generous helping of rice) are imports from mainland Portugal. If you're looking for a fish starter, try limpets (lapas), served in

Below: *One of Madeira's most popular dishes is* espada *(scabbard fish), usually served fried, as here, with bananas, or in wine and garlic.*

Useful Words

apple • *maçã*
baked • *no forno*
beer • *cerveja*
bill • *conta*
boiled • *cozido*
bottle • *garrafa*
bread • *pão*
breakfast • *pequeno almoço*
butter • *manteiga*
dinner • *jantar*
drinks • *bebidas*
eggs • *ovos*
fish • *peixe*
French fries • *friesbatatas fritas*
fried • *frito*
garlic • *alho*
glass • *copo*
grilled • *grelhado*
lemon • *limão*
lunch • *almoço*
meat • *carne*
menu • *ementa*
orange • *laranja*
pepper • *pimento*
red wine • *vinho tinto*
rice • *arroz*
roasted • *asado*
salt • *sal*
shellfish • *mariscos*
stewed • *estufado*
table • *mesa*
tourist menu / fixed-price •
 menu turistica / de preço fixo
white wine • *vinho branco*

their shells in a pool of garlic butter. Of the meat dishes, the most typically Madeiran is *espetada* – skewered chunks of prime beef, rubbed in salt and garlic, garnished with a bay leaf and (to be properly authentic) grilled over a charcoal fire kindled with laurel twigs. **Espetada** is an essential constituent of any village festival, a reminder that, until comparatively recently, meat was reserved for special occasions. Some former staples of the Madeiran diet still appear as **side dishes** – *milho frito* (fried cornmeal), for example, and *pão de batata* (brown bread made with sweet potatoes). Beans (another mainstay of the farm workers' diet) feature prominently in *feijoada* (a nourishing soup almost thick enough to qualify as a casserole). If you're fond of **soups**, look out for *açorda*, made of bread flavoured with garlic and olive oil and with a poached egg as the *coup de grâce*. **Desserts** are usually an 'also ran' in this part of the world, although one can hardly complain when the **fresh fruit** on offer might include anything from mangoes and passion fruit to strawberries, figs and bananas. You may also be offered Madeiran cheesecake (*queijadas da Madeira*) or *bolo de mel*, a dark cake made with honey, molasses, almonds and dried fruit, seasoned with cloves.

Right: *Seafood is in plentiful supply in Madeira's restaurants.*

Above: Beer has been brewed on the island since the 19th century.

Drink

Madeiran fortified **wine** is widely available in restaurants. The drier varieties (Sercial and Verdelho) are generally recommended as apéritifs and should be served chilled (though not ice cold). The smoother Bual goes well with dessert, while Malvasia (Malmsey), the sweetest, should be deferred until coffee. The Portuguese wine, *vinho verde* ('green' referring not to the colour but to the youthfulness), is preferable to the locally produced wine, although great improvements are now being made. **Beer** drinkers may find 'Coral' lager, brewed on Madeira since the 19th century, to their taste. Imported beers are not widely available and are of course much pricier. As a refreshing alternative to beer try the local **cider**, distilled in the southern valleys around Santo da Serra. **Liqueurs** are something of a Madeiran speciality – the choice includes *ginga* (made with cherries), *castanha* (chestnuts), or *amêndoa* (almonds). *Poncha*, made with sugar cane, lemon juice, honey and brandy, should be handled with care! If you don't enjoy alcohol, look out for the refreshing **passion fruit drink**, *brisa maracujá*.

COFFEE LOVERS

The Portuguese are enthusiastic coffee-drinkers and there are numerous ways of saying how you want your coffee served. Ask for **um café** and you'll be given a regular black coffee. If you need something stronger, go for **uma bica**, the closest thing to espresso. Some Madeirans though will prefer it weak (**uma carioca**). Coffee with milk is **café com leite**, but for a really milky coffee you'll want **um galão** (served in a glass). Finally, in the hot summer weather, iced coffee (**café gelado**) goes down a treat.

2
Funchal

The Madeiran capital enjoys a superb setting: a sweeping bay crowned by a diadem of mountain peaks. (The advantages of the natural harbour must have been obvious to the captain discoverers.) The name Funchal derives from *funcho*, the Portuguese for fennel – it is said that Zarco discovered large quantities of this aromatic plant growing on the banks of local rivers. As one Madeiran in two now lives in greater Funchal, it is no surprise that the town corners the lion's share of the tourist trade, most visitors spending at least a few days in the capital before moving on to tour the rest of the island.

For sightseeing purposes, central Funchal is relatively compact and can be comfortably explored on foot. Most things worth seeing can be found in the narrow streets around the 16th-century cathedral (**Sé**) and the **Convento de Santa Clara**. A stroll along the seafront brings two other historic buildings into view: the **Old Customs House** (now the regional parliament) and the **Palácio de São Lourenço**, once the cornerstone of the city's defences. Shopping starts with the famous covered market (**Mercado dos Lavradores**) or the souvenir shops on Avenida Zarco. The best area for eating out, in the evenings especially, is the **Zona Velha** (Old Town), where you can enjoy the twin culinary favourites, *espada* (scabbard fish) and *espetada* (beef or chicken kebab), while listening to *fado*, the Portuguese equivalent of the 'blues'. The **Hotel Zone** at the opposite end of the town has its own bars, restaurants and nightlife, including a casino.

Don't Miss

★★★ Jardim Botânico: subtropical flora in a magnificent setting.
★★★ Adegas de São Francisco: wine lodge famous for its Madeira.
★★★ Sé: the cathedral, one of the oldest buildings on the island.
★★ Quinta das Cruzes: traditional Madeiran villa in beautiful grounds.
★★ Museu de Arte Sacra: art in the former Bishop's Palace.
★★ Zona Velha: Funchal's old quarter – bars, restaurants, traditional *fado* music and the Madeira Story Centre.

Opposite: *The hillsides around Funchal harbour offer spectacular views.*

Nun's Story

The story of one of the 19th-century novices reads like the romantic plot from a Donizetti opera. Maria Clementina, a young woman renowned for her beauty, was browbeaten into entering the convent by her parents, who were unwilling to provide her with a dowry. Just two years later, however, fate came to the rescue when Portugal's new secularist government banned enclosed orders from keeping nuns against their will. Still only 20 years old, Maria promptly fell in love with a handsome army officer. But before they could tie the knot, another change of regime forced her back inside the gates where she languished until her death in 1850, aged 46.

It's possible to see a good deal of the island using Funchal as a base. A cable car now takes visitors up to **Monte** and across to the **Jardim Botânico**, while the inland beauty spots of **Curral das Freiras** and **Boca da Encumeada** are accessible by car. Alternatively there are boat trips exploring the southern coast, from **Cabo Girão** in one direction to **Ponta de São Lourenço** in the other.

TOWN CENTRE
Convento de Santa Clara

Halfway up Calçada de Santa Clara you'll spot the entrance to one of the oldest religious foundations on the island. The Convent of St Clare was founded in 1496 by Zarco's grandson, João Gonçalves de Câmara; his sister, Dona Isabel, was the first abbess. Only the island's wealthiest families sent their daughters here and they expected a spiritual return on their investment. Not all the young ladies went willingly – this was an enclosed order, after all, and the commitment was for life. Happily, today's sisters are all volunteers. You can visit the church on your own but to tour the convent you'll need a guide (allow about 45 minutes). If you have no Portuguese, the sister will make a bold stab at French or English, more

Right: *The cloisters in the Convento de Santa Clara are the oldest part of the building.*

TOWN CENTRE

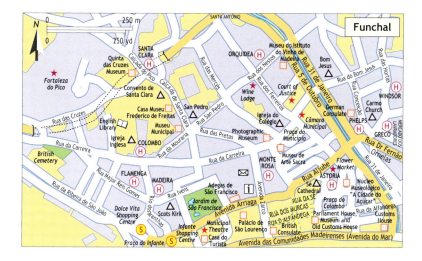

likely a mixture of the two! There's no charge but a small donation is appreciated. **João Gonçalves Zarco**, the discoverer of Madeira, is buried under the high altar where the sanctuary lamps always remain lit. The convent is open daily from 09:00–12:00 and from 15:00–18:00; tel: 291 742 602 (ring the bell).

Quinta das Cruzes ★★

A little way up the hill from the Convento de Santa Clara, on **Calçada do Pico**, Quinta das Cruzes is the archetypal Madeiran **manor house**. If, as is alleged, Zarco built a house here in the 15th century, precious little of it has survived. In the 17th century the estate belonged to the Lomelino family, Genoese wine merchants still commemorated in the chapel. Today's 19th-century mansion has been refurbished from assorted private collections and is open as a **museum**. The furnishings include handsome Regency consoles, and chairs designed by the famous English cabinet-makers, Thomas Chippendale and George Hepplewhite, but probably manufactured on the island. The indigenous craftsmen showed greater ingenuity converting packing cases used for storing sugar into beautifully fashioned cupboards and boxes. If you're not

> **MADEIRA – THE STORY**
>
> One of Madeira's newest attractions, the **Madeira Story Centre** (see page 51), opened in May 2005 at 27–29 Rua D. Carlos I, Funchal. Open daily 10:00–18:00, tel: 291 000 770. Built at a cost of €6.4m (£4.5m), the state-of-the-art exhibition traces the history of the archipelago from its volcanic origins to the present, using interactive games, puzzles, computer simulations, historical artefacts and conventional displays. Afterwards, visitors can relax in the themed café, buy souvenirs in the shop or enjoy the views from the panoramic terrace. For more details, visit their website: www.storycentre.com

bowled over by furniture and silverware, there's Sèvres porcelain, Delft pottery, enamel from Limoges, Chinese vases and Portuguese crib figures to admire. The 19th-century lithographs and watercolours reflect a contemporary fascination with the native flora and fauna, not to mention the scenery, of this dazzling island.

Step into the **garden** to enjoy the floral firework display: hibiscus and bougainvillea, fuchsias and azaleas, dragon trees and Indian laurels, mimosa, eucalyptus, Norfolk Island pines and palm varieties indigenous to Mexico, Malaysia and Colorado. The scattered archaeological remains include a couple of Manueline window frames and what's left of the *pelhourino* – the Funchal pillory. Open Tuesday–Saturday 10:00–12:30 and 14:00–17:30, Sundays 10:00–13:00; tel: 291 740 670.

Igreja Inglesa

Tucked away on Rua do Quebra Costas, the **English Church** is easily missed but worth tracking down. A sedate and seemly reminder of the British presence on the island, it was completed in 1822 to a design by the multi-talented Henry Veitch. The neoclassical style, much in vogue at the time, was also in step with Portuguese law – Protestant churches were not to resemble (or compete with) their Roman Catholic counterparts. Bells were specifically outlawed! During the 1840s the community was torn apart by a bitter sectarian dispute between High and Low Church members of the congregation. The row scandalized Queen Victoria and ultimately led to the founding of a rival chapel. In the

---

PIONEER PHOTOGRAPHER

Portugal's first commercial photographic studio opened in 1865 at Rua da Carreira 43. The original owner, **Vicente Gomes da Silva**, became interested in daguerreotypes after visiting Paris and turned professional in 1852 while still in his twenties. By the time his business folded in 1973, it had passed through four generations of the same family and amassed a priceless archive of more than 380,000 photographs, documenting every conceivable aspect of life on the island. The studio was preserved as a museum and has recently been renovated. **Museu Photographia Vicentes**, open Monday–Friday 10:00–12:00 and 14:00–17:00; tel: 291 225 050.

garden you'll see a bust of Philippa of Lancaster, the mother of one of Portugal's great maritime heroes, Henry the Navigator. The **library** is also open to visitors.

Before the **British Cemetery** was founded in 1765, non-Catholics were buried at sea. The move to the present site on **Rue da Carreira** took place in 1887 – scenically an inspired choice. Read the epitaphs on the mossy headstones and you'll be reminded of the poor souls who arrived on the island already invalids, many of them victims of tuberculosis (see panel, page 89). Open daily 09:00–17:30; tel: 291 211 830.

Opposite: *A coat of arms in the gardens of Quinta das Cruzes.*
Below: *Unusually on Madeira, the English Church was built in the neoclassical style.*

Casa Museu Frederico de Freitas

Turn onto Calçada de Santa Clara and keep an eye out for the **Casa de Calçada**, the town house with the red perimeter wall, opposite the church of São Pedro. Frederico Cunha de Freitas, a lawyer whose lifelong passion was collecting, lived in this 18th-century mansion for many years and on his death left his entire estate, including his priceless collection of antiques, curios and *objets d'art*, to the people of Madeira.

At a first glance, it's hard to believe Dr Freitas found time for anything *but* collecting. The hand-painted *azulejos*, of Persian, Turkish and *Mudéjar* design, date from the 13th–19th centuries and form one of the finest collections of their

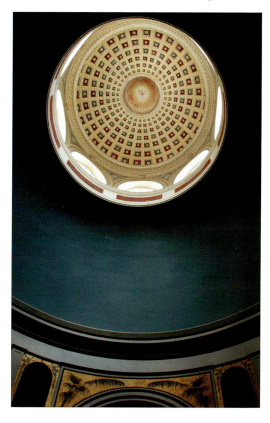

Casa dos Azulejos

Dr Freitas' collection of *azulejos* is exhibited in the recently opened wing alongside the Casa Calçada in the **Museu Freitas**. Apart from hand-painted tiles, you can see mosaics from the Convento de Santa Clara and an accompanying video (in Portuguese only) explaining the art and history of *azulejo* production. There is also a museum café selling tea, coffee and light refreshments.

kind in the world. Religious sculptures from the Portuguese East Indies, paintings, prints and engravings, woodcarvings, antique furniture, porcelain and ceramics (an amazing 2000 milk jugs, teapots and vases) – everything on display reflects the lifelong passion of one extraordinary individual and his travels around the world. Open Tuesday–Saturday 10:00–17:30; tel: 291 220 578.

Museu Municipal

The municipal museum, at Rua da Mouraria 31, is devoted solely to **natural history**. This part of Funchal was once inhabited by Berber slaves from North Africa (Mouraria refers to Moors). The museum was originally the private residence of the Count of Carvahal; it's still known as the **Palácio São Pedro** and is worth seeing in its own right. Most visitors, especially those with children in tow, make a beeline for the **Aquarium**, where the main attractions are the native eels and *garupas*. The natural history collection dates back to the 1850s and, unless you happen to be a vacationing taxidermist, the stuffed sea birds, fossilized corals and nuggets of volcanic rock are unlikely to set the

Below: *Museu Freitas, with the church of São Pedro in the background.*

imagination on fire. Yet it was the patient cataloguing of the island's flora and fauna by local naturalists that paved the way for today's nature reserves and national parks. Open Tuesday–Friday 10:00–18:00, Saturday–Sunday 12:00–18:00; tel: 291 229 761.

Adegas de São Francisco ★★★
The wine lodge, at Avenida Arriaga 28, is now the headquarters of the **Madeira Wine Co.** and a showcase for the island's best-known export. The buildings date from the 17th century and originally belonged to a Franciscan convent (hence the name); in the 1840s they were acquired by the Blandy family. **John Blandy**, a quartermaster with the British garrison during the Napoleonic Wars, arrived on the island in 1807 and started the family wine business four years later.

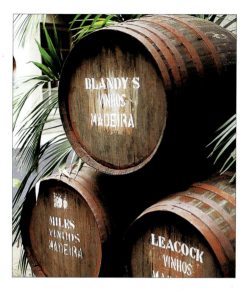

Above: *English families have a long association with Madeira wine.*

The rambling lodge, its whitewashed walls and timber ceilings reeking of old wines, is one of Madeira's top attractions, with more than 200,000 visitors a year. The tour begins in the reception area where you'll see murals by German artist Max Romer celebrating the wine harvest. Through the rustic-looking cobbled courtyard is a covered passageway that was originally a medieval street running down to the harbour. The guide reveals some of the arcane mysteries of the wine-making process. After harvesting, the crop is taken to Funchal for fermentation, a process that takes from four to six weeks. The next stage is known as *estufalgem* (see panel, page 40). The wine is matured in 'warming rooms' or in stainless-steel tanks, heated to a temperature of around 45°C (113°F) and left for at least three months. (Vintage wines, known as *vinhos de canteiro*, are still warmed naturally by the sun's rays.) Each consignment or 'lot' is then left for about two years

> **SLAVES AND MASTERS**
>
> The largest concentration of slaves was in the parishes of Sé (Cathedral) and São Pedro. The majority were indentured not to plantation owners but to noblemen and members of the clergy. They undertook a wide variety of tasks, working in the fields or as clerical assistants, artisans or domestic servants. Women also sold farm produce in the local markets. Unlike the situation on the plantations of the New World, slaves were not purchased in large numbers. One of Madeira's most conspicuous landlords, João Esmeraldo, owned only 14 slaves.

Above: *A view of Funchal's harbour district from the hotel zone.*

ESTUFALGEM

The discovery that *estufalgem* improved Madeiran wines happened quite by accident. It was well known that wine deteriorated in the course of long voyages unless it was fortified with alcohol distilled from cane sugar. But it was not until the second half of the 17th century that connoisseurs noted a marked improvement in wines that had made the long round trip to India. At the time this was attributed to the pitching and tossing motion of the ships, but it was later realized that the warm weather en route was responsible. Wines that had undergone such voyages were promoted as 'round trip' wines (*vinhos de roda*). By the end of the 19th century most producers had switched to the time saving *estufalgem* process of artificial heating in warming rooms or tanks.

to 'rest' in oak casks before blending. It's usually at this stage that the wine is fortified with brandy until it reaches an alcohol level of 18–20%.

In the **museum** you'll see some of the paraphernalia associated with the trade: rough-hewn presses, barrels of formidable girth made from oak or Brazilian satinwood, goatskin wine carriers, hoop irons, etc.

After the tour, there's a short film on the history of wine making and the Blandy connection. Then comes the visit to the tasting rooms and an opportunity to buy. Madeira improves with age – Vintage wine must mature in the cask for a minimum of 20 years and Extra Reserve for 15. It's also extremely durable as professional tasters, allowed the privilege of sampling bottles over 150 years old, eagerly testify. Malvasia (Malmsey) and Verdelho are sweet wines which go well with coffee and dessert. Bual (medium dry) is an excellent complement to soups; while the dry, lightly scented Sercial (which should be served chilled) makes the perfect apéritif. The lodge is open for guided tours only: Monday–Friday 10:30 and 15:30, Saturday 11:00; tel: 291 740 110.

HARBOUR DISTRICT

The **Molhe da Pontinha** (harbour wall) incorporates the old fort of **Nossa Senhora da Conceição**. Gone are the days when rowing boats sailed out to meet the incoming ships anchored off Loo Rock, while young boys dived for coins tossed to them by visitors waiting to be escorted into port. Today, Funchal mainly handles **cruise ships** and the Porto Santo **ferry** (daily sailings from the new quay, *cais nova*) – container ships have been banished to the eastern end of the island. For a 15th-century navigator's eye view, take a trip on the ***Santa Maria***, a replica of Columbus's ship, which makes part of the twice-daily 90-minute journey under sail, weather permitting; tel: 291 220 327, kiosk on Funchal harbour. Helicopters also take off from the harbour on sightseeing tours (Heliatlantis, tel: 291 232 882).

Spread out on the higher ground behind the port are the gentle slopes of the **Parque de Santa Catarina**. A romantic spot for an evening's stroll as the sun sets over the bay, the landscaped gardens are also a good place to bring children. Apart from the play area, there are benches for picnic stops and you can watch the swans glide effortlessly across the lake or luxuriate in the semi-tropical flora. The gardens are named after a **wooden chapel** built on the orders of Zarco's wife, Constança Rodriguez, in 1425. Today's building is a charming 17th-century impostor – only the diminutive bell tower and the water font, decorated with scenes from the life of St Catherine, survive from the Manueline era.

> ### DEEP-SEA FISHING
>
> The fishing season begins in mid-June and continues until early October, weather permitting. During that period boats leave regularly from Funchal Marina in search of bonito, amberjack, dolphin-fish and other species. The best sport, however, is provided by the blue marlin. These streamlined creatures of the deep are a challenge to any hook-and-reel fisherman, being elusive, smart and fast, attaining speeds of up to 45kph (28mph). The female blue marlin is also extremely powerful and can weigh up to 900kg (2000 pounds) – more than six times the average male.

Any roundup of the park's attractions would have to include **Quinta Vigia**, the pink mansion by the lake, now the official residence of the Madeiran president; the sub-tropical gardens of the Casino Park Hotel (designed by the architect of Brasilia, Oscar Niemeyer), and ***The Sower***, an arresting scupture by Francisco Franco.

On the other side of Avenida do Infante is the **Hospício da Princesa**. Now a school, this was originally

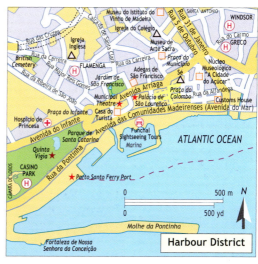

> **JOÃO GONÇALVES ZARCO**
>
> Surprisingly little is known about the founder of Madeira. He was born in Portugal in 1395 but whether in Santarém (northeast of Lisbon), Tomar or Matosinhos, a coastal village north of Porto, is still a matter of debate. On entering the service of Henry the Navigator, Zarco played a prominent role in the Siege of Ceuta in 1415 but lost an eye in the process. Shortly afterwards, according to the Portuguese chronicler, Diogo Gomes, Zarco clashed with Castilian sailors while exploring the coast of West Africa, and it may even have been a Castilian defector who encouraged him to set his sights on **Porto Santo**. Zarco's tenancy of Madeira lasted almost 50 years. At some point during the 1450s, he built a house on the site of what is now **Quinta das Cruzes**. When he died, at the grand old age of 80, he was buried in the **Convent of St Clare** in Funchal.

a sanatorium for patients suffering from tuberculosis. It was founded by the Empress of Brazil to commemorate her daughter, Maria Amélia, who died of the disease in 1853. The dragon trees are the outstanding feature of the gardens.

Avenida Arriaga

The main artery linking the **Sé** (Cathedral) with the **Parque de Santa Catarina**. Leaving Funchal, on the corner of Avenida Zarco you'll see a bronze statue of **João Gonçalves Zarco**, the founding father of Madeira, by Francisco Franco. On your left, opposite the tourist office and the Adegas de São Francisco, are the fortified walls of the **Palácio de São Lourenço**. The keystone of Funchal's defences, São Lourenço was founded early in the 16th century and was still under construction when French corsairs descended on the town in 1566, seizing the fort and massacring the defenders. Refurbished in the 18th century as a palace, São Lourenço's military significance remains – today this is the residence of the military commander. Opposite the **Jardim de São Francisco**, the **Toyota car showroom** hardly deserves its elegant premises. The colonial-style building, formerly the trade halls of the Chamber of Commerce, is decorated with blue and white *azulejos* from the 1920s, depicting scenes from local life including the Monte toboggan run.

Funchal's exquisite **Municipal Theatre** (Teatro Baltasar Dias, tel: 291 211 830) dates from 1888. It's an important venue for plays and other cultural events, including concerts by the Madeira classical orchestra and a **folk music festival** at the end of October. If you get the chance it's definitely

Right: *The 15th-century Chapel of St Catherine was founded by Zarco's wife.*

Above: *The most attractive car showroom in the world?*

worth a look inside to see the gilded private boxes and the beautiful painted ceiling, complete with rubicund cherubs, or *putti*. At the roundabout just before Avenida do Infante is another statue by Francisco Franco, this time commemorating the explorer king, **Henry the Navigator**.

Avenida das Comunidades Madeirenses (Avenida do Mar)

The official name for the esplanade stretching from the **Parque de Santa Catarina** to the **Zona Velha** has proven a bit of a mouthful even for the locals; it's more commonly known as Avenida do Mar. This is the perfect spot for a stroll, before dinner or late on a warm summer night when the main distraction, apart from the rhythmic murmur of the sea, is the **souvenir stalls**, specializing in cheap novelties (miniature bicycles ingeniously fashioned out of twisted wire, etc.) If, like most people, you've left your present-buying to the last minute, you'll find plenty of ideas at the **Casa do Turista**, a showcase for traditional Madeiran handicrafts: embroidery, wickerwork, pottery, glassware and so on.

TAMING FUNCHAL'S RIVERS

Funchal's rivers were once formidable waterways, prone to flooding when swollen by heavy rainfall. In 1803 all three rivers burst their banks with devastating effect: more than 600 people were killed, while dozens of houses and other buildings were destroyed. In the wake of the disaster, a Portuguese military engineer named Reginald Oudinot was called in to make the rivers safe. The stone embankments built by his sappers did the trick and survive to this day.

Above: *Founded in the 16th century, the fortress-palace of São Lourenço still has its own military commander.*

> **MUNICIPAL GARDENS**
>
> Across the road from the theatre on Avenida Arriaga is the **Jardim de São Francisco**. Laid out in the 1870s on the site of a medieval convent, this miniature landscaped park supports a wide variety of subtropical plants and flowers. After brushing up on your flora (purple wreath, golden trumpet, frangipani, Indian lilac, Cape honeysuckle, etc., all labelled) you could take a leisurely stroll among the ponds, fountains and sculptures. A statue of St Francis of Assisi stands in the centre of the gardens. There's also a bandstand and auditorium where concerts and other cultural events are held during the summer months.

The **marina** is a more obvious landmark. From here there are boat excursions to Ribeira Brava in one direction, and Ponta de São Lourenço and Caniçal in the other. Among the floating restaurants moored alongside the marina you'll notice a yacht formerly owned by The Beatles. The legendary pop group christened it 'The Vagrant'. On the landward side, beyond manicured lawns and fountains, is the immaculate façade of the **Palácio de São Lourenço**. The **Old Customs House** on Rua de Alfândega predates it by some years; sadly, few of the original Manueline features have survived the successive restorations. Today the Customs House is the headquarters of the regional parliament. Funchal's rivers, now tamed and prettified by trailing bougainvillea, are relatively inconspicuous but you'll spot two of them carving their way through the town from a point near the end of the avenue.

Núcleo Museológico 'A Cidade do Açúcar'

Given the importance of 'white gold' in Madeira's history, a museum devoted to the **sugar trade** is only to be expected. But the site on Praça do Colombo 5 is famous for another reason. The original 15th-century house (demolished in the 1870s) belonged to a wealthy Flemish sugar merchant named Jennin Esmerandt. One of Esmerandt's friends, it turns out, was none other than Christopher Columbus, who stayed here on at least one occasion. The foundations of Esmerandt's house were excavated in 1989 to reveal the remains of an old cistern. Other finds open a window onto life at the time, not only the coins, buttons, fragments of porcelain, metal weights, beads, goats' teeth and rats' bones, but the remnants of food (nuts, cherry stones, grape seeds, a shredded pineapple kernel) – each tells its own story. In the adjoining room you'll see maps, charts and artefacts connected with the sugar trade, including the distinctive conical moulds which feature on Funchal's coat of arms to this day. Open Monday–Friday 10:00–12:30 and 14:00–18:00; tel: 291 236 910.

Sé ★★★

Funchal Cathedral on Largo da Sé dates from the same period as the Old Customs House and the Convento de Santa Clara. It was completed in 1514 under the patronage of Manuel I, whose reign coincided with the discovery of the Americas, earning him the soubriquet 'fortunate'. The cathedral is an early example of **Manueline architecture**, a uniquely Portuguese blend of Gothic and Renaissance styles, characterized among other things by exuberant sculptural decoration – the sailor's knot motif on the pinnacles of the east end is a typical ornamental embellishment. The architect, Pêr Annes, hailed from the Alentejo in southern Portugal where Moorish influences were still strong; this explains

> ### FESTIVAL ROUND-UP
>
> The most important village festivals are mentioned in the text. The following is a summary. All the events below take place in Funchal unless otherwise indicated.
>
> • **January:** New Year firework display is among the most spectacular in Europe.
> • **February:** Rio-inspired Carnival procession and fancy dress parade with music and dancing into the small hours.
> • **April:** Flower Festival (see panel, page 48).
> • **June:** *Fins de Semana Musicais* (Musical Weekends). Concerts of classical music featuring top Madeiran performers.
> • **August:** Feast of the Assumption (15 August). Religious festival celebrated all over the island but especially in Monte.
> • **September:** Grape Harvest. Bacchanalian revels in Funchal, also villages across the island.
> • **December:** Christmas. Highlights include street illuminations (using three-quarters of a million light bulbs) and crib displays.

Left: *Children play an important role in Funchal's annual carnival procession.*

AVIATORS

Visitors to **Parque de Santa Catarina** will notice a statue commemorating two Portuguese aviators, Gago Coutinho and Sacadura Cabral. The two naval officers made the first air crossing from Lisbon to Madeira in March 1921. This pioneering journey was a test run for the maiden transatlantic flight from Lisbon to Rio de Janeiro the following year. Flying a Rolls-Royce-powered Fairey flying boat and using a revolutionary new sextant developed by Coutinho himself, the duo set off on 30 March 1922 and were in sight of the Brazilian coast when they were forced to ditch after running out of fuel. The Portuguese navy despatched another flying boat and the intrepid pair resumed their odyssey, but were again forced to ditch. They eventually arrived in Rio on 17 June, piloting their third aircraft.

other decorative touches like the *azulejo* tiles on the spire. The simple, almost minimalist, façade is more in keeping with a village church than a cathedral – only the coat of arms of King Manuel above the portal hints at the building's status. The interior also holds a surprise or two. Allow your eyes time to adjust to the gloom, then gaze upward at the carved ceiling, among the finest in Portugal. Fashioned from native cedar wood and overlaid with ivory, the mesmerizing geometric patterns are a typical Arab device. As you stroll down the nave towards the apse, you'll be amazed by the painted arabesques on the vaults, as engaging as the tangled borders of an illuminated manuscript. The paintings on the gilded reredos are by 17th-century Portuguese artists. Don't leave without taking a closer look at the carvings in the choir stalls. The work of 17th-century Flemish craftsmen, they're a witty commentary on urban life of the period with nattily dressed merchants standing in for the apostles. Open from Monday–Saturday 07:00–13:00, 16:00–19:00, Sunday 08:00–20:30; tel: 291 228 155.

PRAÇA DO MUNICIPIO

There are several reasons for making a short detour to Funchal's busy **main square**. If you haven't done so already, this is your chance to visit the **Museu de Arte Sacra**. Alternatively, cross the square's wavy mosaic floor to the **Igreja do Colégio**, otherwise known as the Church of St John the Evangelist. Designed by a Portuguese architect, Bras Fernandes, it was completed in 1629, almost 60 years after members of the Jesuit Order first arrived on Madeira. The statues on the austere Baroque façade are of St Ignatius Loyola, St Francis Xavier, St Stanislaus and St Francis Borgia, four outstanding figures in the Order. The church is

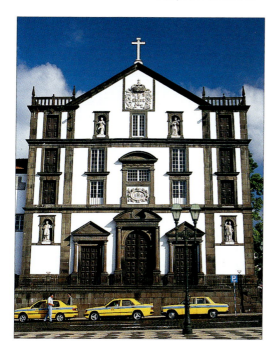

Left: *Founded by the Jesuits, the Igreja do Colégio overlooks Funchal's main square, Praça do Municipio.*
Opposite: *Manueline doorway on the façade of Funchal Cathedral.*

open only for services; if you get the chance, take a look at the retable behind the high altar – the woodcarvings, overlaid with gold leaf, are reckoned to be among the finest in Portugal. The adjacent buildings are now part of the University of Madeira.

Funchal's handsome town hall (**Câmara Municipal**) is on the opposite side of the square. The original owner was a Portuguese nobleman, who commissioned it as his private residence in 1758. The exquisite marble statue of Leda and her swan in the courtyard is more appealing than the lacklustre local history museum upstairs.

Museu de Arte Sacra ★★

The Museum of Sacred Art, on the corner of Rua do Bispo and Praço do Municipio, is a cultural treat which should not be missed. Of the original Bishop's Palace, completed around 1600, only the chapel and the covered balcony

---

BOAT EXCURSIONS

Taking a boat trip is both enjoyable in itself and an excellent and energy-saving way of exploring the Madeiran coastline. Most of the companies listed below operate from Funchal Marina. Destinations include Ribeira Brava, Ponta do Sol and Baia de Abra (near Prainha).
Marina do Funchal: tel: 291 232 717, fax: 291 225 521.
Albatroz Organization: Marina do Funchal, tel: 963 003 864.
Costa do Sol: Marina do Funchal, tel: 291 224 390, fax: 291 235 735.
Santa Maria, Actividades Marítimo-Turísticas: Marina do Funchal, tel/fax: 291 220 327.
Quinta da Bela Vista ('Gavião'): tel: 291 706 400, fax: 291 706 401, website: www.belavistamadeira.com

facing the square (best viewed from the window between floors) survived the earthquake of 1748; the Baroque reconstruction was completed nine years later. The exhibition is spread over two floors and can be viewed comfortably in a couple of hours. The collection of embroidered vestments and liturgical silverware, assembled from religious foundations across Madeira, is remarkable given the size of the island. Look out for the gold-plated processional cross, presented to the chapter of Funchal Cathedral by King Manuel I (1495–1521). The Portuguese paintings date from the 16th–18th centuries. Several of Madeira's founding families were artistic patrons; Grão Vasco's splendid *Adoration of the Magi*, for example, was financed by a prominent member of the Teixeira clan, while the descendants of Zarco himself crop up in the panels of a triptych ostensibly commemorating SS James and Philip. The majority of Madeira's patrons, though, were sharp-eyed merchants who had amassed huge fortunes from the sugar trade and were looking to build new reputations for themselves as men of taste – the Italian, Simon Acciaiuoli, for example, who appears with his wife in a *Descent from the Cross*. The museum's small but remarkable collection of Flemish art is founded on works now reliably attributed to Dirk Bouts, Gerard David, Jan Provost and Joost van Cleve, painters of repute who have earned a place in the world's leading galleries. Open Tuesday–Saturday 10:00–12:30 and 14:30–18:00, Sunday 10:00–13:00; tel: 291 228 900.

Museu do Instituto do Vinho de Madeira

Not far from the Praça do Município, on Rua 5 de Outubro (no. 78) you'll see an imposing building with a tall watchtower. It's the headquarters of the **Madeira Wine Institute**, the ultimate authority responsible for all aspects

---

FLOWER FESTIVAL

A colourful event in the Madeiran calendar, the Flower Festival takes place over two days in April or early May. The children's costume procession launches the weekend's celebrations that culminate in the building of a floral 'wall of hope' (*muro de esperança*) in the **Praça do Município**. The street parade held the next day showcases Madeira's flora and handicrafts. The procession starts at the **Parque de Santa Catarina** and follows **Avenida Arriaga**, ending in the Largo do Colégio (details from tourist information). Prime vantage points, such as the balcony of the Golden Gate Café, are snapped up weeks in advance.

of production and quality control. Those precious bottles of Sercial or Verdelho you've bought as presents for friends – or for your own consumption – will already have received the *selo de garantia* (seal of authentication) from the institute. A small but engaging **museum** traces the history of wine production on the island, mainly through photographs, prints and engravings, although you'll also see examples of wine presses and barrel-making equipment (a cooper is occasionally on hand to demonstrate the craft). The explanations are thorough and will appeal particularly to wine buffs.

Appropriately enough, the building was formerly the home of wine merchant, Henry Veitch. He designed it himself and it became the prototype for colonial residences in India, South Africa and Mozambique. It is open Monday–Friday 09:00–18:00; tel: 291 204 600.

Opposite: *Originally the Bishop's Palace, the Museu de Arte Sacra has a distinguished art collection.*
Below: *Bougainvilleas contribute to Madeira's colourful floral displays by flowering throughout the year.*

Mercado dos Lavradores

Funchal's indoor produce market is on **Rua Dr Fernão Ornelas** on the edge of the Zona Velha. It was built in the early 1940s in the regional style known as 'Novo Estado' and with the customary *azulejo* decoration. The best time to visit is on Friday or Saturday when farmers from all over Madeira trundle into town with truckloads of **fruit and vegetables**. Enjoy listening to the banter and soak up the colours – the **flower sellers** are here in force, wearing their distinctive candy-striped skirts and red waistcoats. So are the island's **fishermen** with their catches of tuna, scabbard and shellfish. If you're shopping for

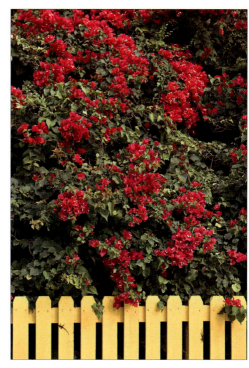

MARITIMO FOOTBALL

Funchal's highly successful football team plays at the **Estádio dos Barreiros** (Barreiros Stadium), Rua Dom Carlos, tel: 291 205 000, fax: 291 222 939. Most games take place on Sunday afternoons or weekday evenings. Tickets are sold at the ground on match days and at other times from the club museum or shop (Rua Dom Carlos I, 14).

HORSE RIDING

Horse riding opportunities are limited, but do exist:
Terras de Aventura, Caminho do Amparo 25, 900-248, Funchal, tel: 291 708 990, fax: 291 708 999.
Horse riding is also offered at the **Estrelicia, Buganvilia, Mimosa** and **Florassol** hotels (Dorisol chain), tel: 291 706 670, fax: 291 706 680.

a picnic, look out for the small, sweet bananas – Madeira is one of only two native producers within the EU (the Canaries is the other). If you've worked up an appetite, there are snack bars *in situ*, or you can head for one of the cafés in the Old District. Open Monday–Thursday 07:00–16:00, Friday 07:00–20:00, Saturday 07:00–15:00, closed Sunday.

ZONA VELHA **

Funchal's '**Old Quarte**r' lies east of the modern town and dates back to the early 16th century. At that time it was known as 'Santa Maria' after a church which no longer exists but is still commemorated in the street name, Rua de Santa Maria. For a long time this was a run-down part of Funchal inhabited by the poorest Madeirans. Nowadays, it's a prettified **pedestrianized zone** with cobblestones, antique gas lamps and brightly painted house fronts. After sundown, prospective diners are lured by the aromas of Portuguese fish stews and the plaintive strains of *fado* music emanating from the pavement cafés.

Beyond the **Capela do Corpo Santo** (on Rua de Santa Maria), founded by local fishermen at the end of the 15th century, is a larger church, the **Igreja do Socorro**. Take a peek inside at the splendid Baroque chancel arch – it chimes surprisingly well with the gaudily decorated altarpieces.

On the seaward side of these two monuments, the custard-yellow walls of the **Fortaleza de São Tiago** are the Zona Velha's most obvious landmark. The work of a Portuguese military engineer, Jerónimo Jorge, it was completed in 1637 and later enlarged. It looks tame now that the marauding pirates have retreated for good, along with the garrison, leaving behind nothing more threatening than palms and potted plants. Inside there's a tiny **Museum of Contemporary Art** (Portuguese paintings from the 1960s onwards) and not much else, though there are great views of the harbour from the battlements. Open Monday–Saturday 10:00–12:30 and 14:00–17:30; tel: 291 226 456. Just below is a stony beach, **Praia da Barreirinha**. You can swim here (the locals do) but you may prefer the **seawater lido** just beyond the fort and accessible from the road by lift. The attendants will point you in

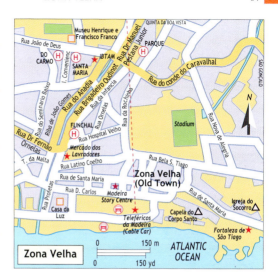

the direction of the changing rooms and snack bars, where you can buy sandwiches, soft drinks and beer. The pool terraces are safe for children and there's a lifeguard on duty.

Madeira Story Centre **

The Madeira Story Centre (see panel, page 35) gives an overview of 14 million years of history, during a visit that can last well over an hour. It covers the entire period from geological genesis to modern times and does so in a way that takes the visitor back in time with the aid of authentic artefacts and multimedia audio-visual displays – combining history with an entertaining cultural experience.

And when history becomes too much, chill out on the terrace, take a coffee in the themed café, or visit the tasteful and well-stocked souvenir shop. Open daily 10:00–18:00; tel: 291 000 770.

IBTAM

The initials stand for the **Institute of Embroidery, Tapestry and Handicrafts**, the body that regulates Madeira's traditional cottage industries. The museum, at Rua do Visconde de Anadia 44, concentrates on embroidery and will appeal

Opposite: *Farmers from across the island converge on Funchal's Mercado dos Lavradores (Workers' Market).*

THE JESUITS

The first Jesuit missionaries arrived on Madeira in 1569 following an invitation from King Sebastião of Portugal. Only a year later, French corsairs murdered their leader, Inácio de Azevedo. Undeterred, the shock troops of the Counter Reformation returned in 1572 with a charter to found a monastery and college (now the university). Substantial landowners, the order played a major role in wine cultivation, introducing new grape varieties such as Bual and Sercial on their estates around Fajã dos Padres.

Henry Veitch

One of Madeira's most colourful figures, Veitch was born in 1782 in Selkirk, although, according to one acquaintance, he shed all traces of his Scottish origins. Veitch made his fortune as a wine merchant supplying the Portuguese navy with Sercial. A sometime British consul, he was a constant embarrassment to the motherland on account of his womanizing and extravagant lifestyle. Churchgoers were scandalized by the shenanigans at his parties and by his endless succession of mistresses. In his spare time, Veitch was no mean architect, designing the **English Church**, the house on Rua 5 de Outubro (now the **Madeira Wine Institute**) and the **Quinta do Jardim da Serra** where he and his second wife are buried.

mainly to devotees interested in stitching and design. The displays date back to the late 19th century, when almost every able bodied woman on the island was embroidering bedspreads, tablecloths etc. to order. Open Monday–Friday 10:00–12:30 and 14:00–17:30; tel: 291 223 141.

Museu Henrique e Francisco Franco

Around the corner from IBTAM, on Rua João de Deus, look for an unusual building with a cylindrical bastion. It dates from the 1940s and was designed for the brothers, Henrique (a painter) and Francisco (a sculptor) Franco de Sousa. The Francos were born in Funchal and attended art school in Lisbon where they spent most of their working lives. Both benefited from the creative hothouse that was Paris in the 1920s and particularly from friendships with Picasso and Modigliani. The museum exhibits assorted landscapes and portraits by Henrique and sculptures by the more gifted Francisco whose commissions in Funchal include the monuments to Zarco and Henry the Navigator and the sculpture *The Sower* in the Parque de Santa Catarina. Open Monday–Friday 10:00–12:30 and 14:00–18:00; tel: 291 230 633.

Quinta da Boa Vista

Just outside Funchal, on Lombo da Boa Vista, are the Boa Vista ('Fine View') **orchid nurseries**, founded in the 1960s by a retired British fighter pilot and his wife, herself the daughter of a world authority on these beautiful flowers. The underlying philosophy of the Boa Vista enterprise is to preserve and propagate species otherwise threatened with extinction.

Thriving among the cymbidiums, cattleyas and slipper orchids (paphiopediums) are equally colourful displays of strelitzias, anthuriums, Latin American bromeliads and aloes. The nurseries are open Tuesday–Saturday 10:00–12:30 and 14:00–18:00, and are best seen from late November to the end of April; tel: 291 220 468.

HOTEL ZONE

This ribbon development of hotels and apartments to the west of Funchal starts near the **Parque de Santa Catarina** and continues for 5km (3 miles) in the direction of **Câmara de Lobos**. To walk into town from here can take anything from 30 minutes to an hour (don't be fooled by the brochures), but there's plenty of transport available – a regular bus service as well as taxis. The hotels advertise their cliff-top locations, sea views, lush green subtropical gardens and comprehensive sports and leisure facilities.

MADEIRA MAGIC

One of the island's newest attractions, this **theme park** in the heart of Funchal's hotel zone has been designed for the enjoyment of adults and children alike. A guided tour around the gardens offers visitors an unusual introduction to the botanical history of the island, which boasts sub-tropical vegetation and flora from every part of the globe. For the kids there's interactive science, planetarium shows, 3D wildlife animations and plenty of space to run around in. The amenities include a restaurant, tea room, health club and baby-changing facilities, also disabled access. **Rua Ponto da Cruz**, São Martinho, Funchal, tel: 291 700 708, website: www.madeira-magic.com Open Tuesday–Friday 10:00–18:00, Saturday and Sunday 10:00–19:00.

Opposite: *The Fortaleza de São Tiago.*

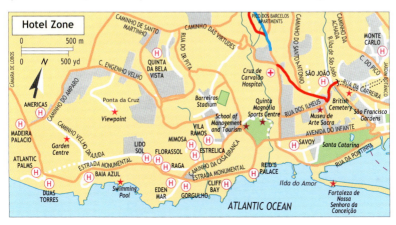

Cycling

While Madeira's mountainous terrain hardly gives encouragement to amateur cyclists, Porto Santo is much easier to negotiate. To promote the sport on the island, the Madeira Sports Association organizes a round-the-island cycle race every July, about 50 riders taking part. Back on Madeira, Funchal town council has finally approved a scheme for a cycle lane on the Estrada Monumental, the highway which links the town centre with the hotel district and the beach at Praia Formosa.

Below: *The new motorway linking Funchal with Madeira International airport has cut journey times considerably.*

On the subject of views, it's only a short drive to one of Funchal's finest vantage points, **Pico dos Barcelos**.

The most luxurious swimming pool is at the **Savoy Hotel** but the facilities at the public **lido** – an olympic pool with sea access, children's pool, etc. – will meet the needs of most families. There's a diving club based at the **Pestana Palms Hotel** (Rua do Gorgulho 17, tel: 291 709 200), near the beach at **Praia Formosa** and tennis and squash courts (and swimming pool) in the lovely surroundings of the Quinta Magnólia municipal gardens.

Quinta Magnólia

A former country club, Quinta Magnólia is on Rua do Dr Pita – follow the road north from Reid's Palace Hotel. Since 1980 it has been a **public park**, managed by the Madeiran regional government. You can make use of the plentiful sporting amenities (of which more later) or relax in the rambling subtropical gardens dreamt up by the original owner, the former American consul, and keen amateur botanist, T H Marsh. The villa is now home to the School of Hotel Management and Tourism – good news for visitors, as the students rustle up a four-course set lunch and afternoon tea at pleasingly affordable prices. (Book at least 24 hours ahead as tables are at a premium.) If you're the sporty type you'll be more interested in the tennis and squash courts, open-air heated swimming pool, putting green and jogging track. All the facilities are open to the public and there's a playground to keep the children amused. Open daily from 08:00–21:00.

Reid's Palace Hotel

Reid's sits sedate and solitary on the rocky promontory it has occupied for more than a hundred years, as immovable as a dowager settled into her favourite armchair and equally implacable in the face of change. Like Raffles in Singapore, Reid's has become an institution to the point where it's hard to imagine Madeira without it.

William Reid was the son of a near destitute Scottish crofter. He arrived in Funchal in 1836 with five pounds in his pocket and a burning ambition to succeed. From hiring out *quintas* to wealthy invalids, he moved on to hotels. Reid's was his dream and though he died a few years before the doors opened for the first time in 1891, his notion of what a luxury hotel should be lives on. While no longer *de rigeur*, guests tend to dress for dinner here, and afternoon tea is still served on the terrace with cucumber sandwiches, scones and clotted cream. And while every luxury hotel has its spa, heated swimming pools (there are three), saunas (two) and gourmet restaurants (four), how many can boast a library or a billiards room? Were Sir Winston Churchill – a guest during the 1950s when he was recuperating from a stroke – to return today, one can imagine him feeling at home here. The same can probably be said for the other celebrities who have dropped in over the years: deposed emperors (Karl von Habsburg), former despots (General Batista of Cuba), poets (Maria Rainer Rilke), dramatists (George Bernard Shaw, who famously took dancing lessons, though well into his seventies), film stars (Gregory Peck and Roger Moore), missionaries (Albert Schweitzer), not forgetting British prime ministers (Lloyd George, Anthony Eden and Churchill). Madonna? – Reid's awaits!

Above: *A view of the luxurious Reid's Palace Hotel.*

BEST FLOWER BUYS

For cut flowers, visit the stalls outside **Funchal Cathedral** or **Mercado dos Lavradores**. Orchids are the speciality of the **Quinta da Boa Vista** and the **Jardim Orquídea** (Pregetters), and bulbs, plants and flowers are on sale in the **Magnolia Flower Shop**, in the gardens of the Casino Park Hotel. **A Estufa**, Madeira's largest commercial flower producer, packages flowers and plants for shipment by air. They have branches in Funchal (Rua do Castanheiro 39 and Centro Comercial da Sé), the hotel zone (Eden Mar Hotel, Rua do Gorgulho) and Caniço.

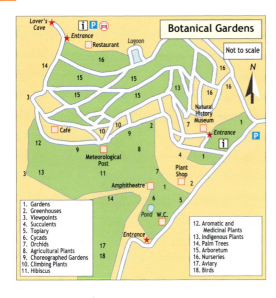

Jardim Botânico ★★★

Take bus no. 29, 30 or 31 from the centre of Funchal to **Caminho do Meio** and the Botanical Gardens, one of Madeira's star attractions (access from Monte via cable car). The mansion in the former private estate, **Quinta de Bom Successo**, is now a small **Natural History Museum**. The gardens, spread over 5ha (12 acres) of terraced hillside, are dedicated to the cultivation and conservation of more than 2000 species of plants, trees and flowers from every continent. The exhibits are divided by region and genus and labelled in Latin and Portuguese (not English, unfortunately). There's something intoxicating about a place where everything thrives and proliferates, as here, where the warm air is heady with exotic fragrances. Among the flowers, you'll encounter azaleas, arum lilies, orchids and bromeliads, Japanese camellias, 'birds of paradise' (strelitzia), and Mexican 'tears of Christ'. It's hard to miss the palm garden and the towering giant known as *Phoenix canariensis*, while across the way, in the arboretum, are jacarandas, prickly dragon trees, ginkgos, sequoias and the majestic *Araucaria australiensis*, which can grow up to 60m (200ft) in its natural habitat.

One of the main purposes of the gardens is to breed and conserve plants indigenous to Madeira's coastline and laurel forest – geraniums and marguerites, wild orchids, and rare members of the subtropical *Cycadales* family, for example. These are gardens with something for everyone; depending on your taste, the highlight might be the cactus or rose garden, the herbarium with its stock of medicinal and aromatic plants, or the pergolas, cascades and escarpments.

Madeira Wine Rally

Car rally enthusiasts rate this challenging annual event as one of the best tarmac competitions anywhere. High profile drivers from all over Europe take part – previous winners include Piero Liatti and Bruno Thiry. This gruelling stage of the European Automobile Championship circuit takes place during the first week in August. Contact the tourist office in Funchal for more details.

Agriculture is a special focus of study, which explains the abundance of tea plants, sweet potato and fruit trees. Whichever path you take there are numerous vantage points with sweeping views of Funchal and the coast. The gardens are open daily 09:00–18:00; tel: 291 211 200; website: www.madeirabotanicalgarden.com Amenities include a café and shop.

Just below the gardens (separate entrance, same ticket) is the **Jardim dos Loiros**. From the squawks, screams and insane chattering you'll conclude (rightly) that this is a bird park – and a 'must see' if you have children. The preening stars are the parrots, lories and conures, but they're all rumbustious extroverts, from the Australian parakeets and the absurd Ghanaian hornbills to the mynah birds, cockatoos, lovebirds and macaws. Bring earplugs!

Take the side turning below the bird park (Rua Pita da Silva) and after 100m you'll come to the **Jardim Orquídea**, the orchid nurseries of the Pregetter family. Strictly speaking the plants here bloom year-round, but for the best displays come between November and early April. There are more than 400 varieties of orchid, including rare native species like *Dachtylorhiza foliosa* and equally colourful imports from Brazil, India and New Guinea. You can watch them being cultivated in the laboratory before shopping for a plant to take home as a memento of your visit. Open daily 09:00–18:00.

> **SOCCER STAR**
>
> Harry Hinton was 18 when, in 1875, he made history by organizing the first soccer game in Portugal. It took place in Camacha, next to the Café O Relógio (a wall plaque now commemorates the event). Hinton remained closely associated with the game for the rest of his life. He was present in 1910 at the historic opening match between the newly formed Madeiran club, Marítimo, and an English scratch team (the Portuguese creating a minor sensation by winning 2–1). Hinton provided a cup in his name in the 1920s and was made honorary president of Marítimo in 1942. Today the club, which plays at the Estádio dos Barreiros in Funchal, is one of the strongest sides in the Portuguese first division.

Below: *Topiary Garden, one of the delights in the Jardim Botânico.*

Funchal at a Glance

BEST TIMES TO VISIT

Weather-wise, Funchal is pleasant at any time of year. July, August and September are the sunniest months, though September can be wet. It's warm in June but there's more cloud. August is the busiest month as many mainland visitors arrive for the summer vacation. The Christmas season (8 December to 6 January) is especially lively, with street and harbour illuminations, concerts, crib displays and one of Europe's most spectacular firework displays to mark New Year.

GETTING THERE

Road links between the airport (tel: 291 524 322) and Funchal are good. A taxi will take about 25 minutes to cover the 16km (10 miles). There is a bus service, but it's not very reliable (journey time is around 45 minutes).

GETTING AROUND

Funchal is easily negotiated on foot but be prepared for some uphill walking. There are two **bus** stations (eastbound and westbound) for accessing other parts of the island. (Timetables and destination information are available from tourist offices.) Town buses are orange. Tourist passes (valid for your stay) are a good idea if you intend making frequent use of buses. They are on sale from kiosks on Avenida do Mar, where you will also find bus stops. **Taxis** are metered but there are fixed rates for out-of-town journeys – check with the driver about prices.

WHERE TO STAY

LUXURY
Reid's Palace, Estrada Monumental 139, tel: 291 717 171, fax: 291 717 177, website: www.reidspalace.com Colonial-style luxury, Reid's is an institution, the emphasis being on tradition and formality. Offers generous out-of-season packages.
Savoy, Avenida do Infante, tel: 291 213 000, fax: 291 223 103, website: www.savoyresort.com The Savoy's facilities rival those of Reid's, the swimming pool having the edge.
Cliff Bay Resort Hotel, Estrada Monumental 147, tel: 291 707 700, fax: 291 762 525, website: www.portobay.com 5-star facilities include outdoor and indoor pools, health club, tennis courts and sauna.
Quintinha de São João, Rua da Levada de São João 4, tel: 291 740 920, website: www.quintinhasaojoao.com Just a short way out of town, but complete with spa, gymnasium and two pools, as well as excellent restaurant.
Quinta da Bela Vista, Caminho Avista Navios 4, tel: 291 706 400, fax: 291 706 401, website: www.belavistamadeira.com About 15 minutes from the centre by car, has a delightful garden setting.

MID-RANGE
Orquídea, Rua dos Netos 71, tel: 291 200 120, fax: 291 227 157, website: www.hotelorquidea.com Modern hotel, excellent facilities and a roof terrace with views of Funchal.
Eden Mar, Rua do Gorgulho 2, tel: 291 709 700, fax: 291 761 966. Excellent amenities including a huge pool, a sauna and a jacuzzi.
Windsor, Rua das Hortas 4, tel: 291 233 081, fax: 291 233 080, website: www.hotelwindsorgroup.pt Friendly hotel in excellent downtown location, with small rooftop swimming pool.

BUDGET
Pension Astoria, Rua João Gago 10, tel/fax: 291 227 229, website: www.pensaoastoria.com The location can hardly be bettered; clean and well run but only some rooms have bathrooms.

WHERE TO EAT

LUXURY
A Morgadinha, Rua da Levada de São João 4 (next to Quintinha de São João), tel: 291 740 920. This hotel-restaurant is not easy to find, but worth the trouble for the wonderful dishes.
Casa Velha, Rua Imperatriz D. Amélia 69, tel: 291 225 749. Expensive, but superb food, creative menu.
Les Faunes, Reid's Palace, tel: 291 717 171. *Haute cuisine* at prices to match, smart

Funchal at a Glance

dress is essential. Advance reservations from www.reidspalace.com

MID-RANGE
Arsénio's, Rua de Santa Maria 169, tel: 291 224 007. Seafood restaurant, known for its *fado* music, caters for tourists.
Doca de Cavacas, Estrada Monumental, Ponta da Cruz, tel: 291 762 057. Restaurant in hotel district serving attractively priced seafood dishes, including *espada* (scabbard fish).
Gavião Novo, Rua de Santa Maria 131, tel: 291 229 238. Small family-owned restaurant rustling up tasty and reasonably priced Madeiran fare. Reservations advised.
O Jango, Rua de Santa Maria 166, tel: 291 221 280. Cosy, and popular with locals and visitors; fresh fish a speciality.
O Tapassol, Rua Dom Carlos I 62, tel: 291 225 023. Restaurant with rooftop terrace serving Madeiran dishes.

BUDGET
Golden Gate Café, Avenida Arriaga 29, tel: 291 234 383. This colonial-era café sells everything from cakes and pastries to more refined Portuguese cuisine.

SHOPPING

Casa do Turista (Avenida do Mar) is the main outlet for souvenirs, otherwise try **Rua João Tavira** and other streets around the cathedral. There are three main shopping centres: Eden Mar (Rua do Gorgulho) in the hotel zone, Dolce Vita (western end of Avenida Arriaga) and Infante (Avenida Arriaga) near the marina.

TOURS AND EXCURSIONS

Strawberry World Island Tours, Rua do Gorgulho Loja 25, Funchal, tel: 291 762 421, website: www.strawberry-world.com Half- and full-day tours of the island with commentary and fluent English-speaking guides.
Madeira Explorers, Monumental Lido, tel: 291 763 701, website: www.madeira-levada-walks.com
Most **bus companies** arrange excursions to tourist attractions (*see* bus stations for details). For outdoor activities contact **Terras de Aventura & Turismo**, Caminho do Amparo 25, tel: 291 776 818, fax: 291 771 018.
Heliatlantis offers bird's-eye tours of Funchal and the island by helicopter; tel: 291 232 882, fax: 291 232 804, or go to Estrada do Pontinha (Cais dos Contentores), between the marina and the harbour.

USEFUL CONTACTS

Tourist Offices: Funchal, Avenida Arriaga 16, tel: 291 211 900, fax: 291 232 151, website: www.madeira-tourism.org Open Monday–Friday 09:00–20:00, Saturday and Sunday 09:00–18:00; **CC Monumental Lido**, Estrada Monumental 284, tel: 291 775 254. Open Monday–Friday 09:00–20:00, Saturday and Sunday 09:00–14:00.
Funchal Harbour, Molhe da Pontinha, tel: 291 281 743 (only open for cruise ships).
Car rental:
Avis, Madeira International airport, tel: 291 524 392. Also at Largo António 164, Funchal, tel: 291 764 546; **Hertz**, Madeira International airport, tel: 291 523 040. Also at Rua Ivens 12, tel: 291 226 026 and Estrada Monumental 284, tel: 291 764 410.
Motorcycle, scooter and bike hire: Joyride CC Olimpo Shop, 210–211 Avenida do Infante, Funchal, tel/fax: 291 234 906.
Diving: Scorpio Divers, Complexo Balnear do Lido 9000, Funchal, tel: 291 766 977; Golfinho Diving Centre, Cliff Bay Resort Hotel, Estrada Monumental, tel: 291 707 700, fax: 291 762 525, website: www.portobay.com
Tennis: Rua Dr Pita, Anexo Barreiros, tel: 291 763 237, fax: 291 763 930.
Horse Riding: Terras de Aventura, Caminho do Amparo 25, tel: 291 708 990, fax: 291 708 999.
Sailing: Costa do Sol Marina do Funchal, tel: 291 224 390, fax: 291 235 735; Nautisantos Sport Fishing Madeira Marina do Funchal, tel/fax: 291 231 312, website: www.nautisantosfishing.com
Dolphin and whale watching excursions: Katherine B, Travessa Das Virtudes 23, São Martinho, 9000-163 Funchal, tel: 291 952 685, fax: 291 752 689.

3
Western Madeira

Western Madeira is possibly the least known part of the island. One reason is that until fairly recently it was remote and inaccessible – for example, until the 1960s, the beautiful coastal hamlet of **Paúl do Mar** (now the island's surfing 'capital') could be reached only by boat. Everything changed in 1997 with the opening of the **Via Rapida** between Funchal and **Ribeira Brava**, cutting the journey time from one hour to just 15 minutes. Coach tours and boat excursions visit this busy little resort. Beyond Ribeira Brava the coast road threads through remarkably fertile countryside, over hillsides planted with bananas and vines. Along the way you can experience the famous sunsets at **Ponta do Sol**, visit the lighthouse at **Ponta do Pargo** (the island's most westerly point), or stop for lunch at one of several picturesque fishing villages – **Jardim do Mar** for example. Another strong suit of the region is its churches and chapels, many of them off the beaten track but worth exploring for their architecture, artistic treasures and splendid *Mudéjar* ceilings.

The main road north from Ribeira Brava follows the course of Madeira's most impressive river valley, climbing to the *miradouro* (lookout) at **Encumeada** and the fringes of the **Paúl da Serra** plateau before making the spectacular descent to **São Vicente**. The coastal scenery here, towards the resort village of **Porto Moniz**, is breathtaking. Awesome Atlantic breakers pound the basalt beaches, flooding the coves and rocky inlets and submerging the treacherous reefs, a perennial hazard to shipping in the area.

Don't Miss

★★★ **Boca da Encumeada:** *miradouro* with views of the north coast and Serra de Agua.
★★★ **Rabaçal:** enchanting scenery as well as good *levada* walking.
★★ **Grutas de São Vicente:** volcanic caves formed more than 400,000 years ago.
★★ **Porto Moniz:** coastal resort with swimming pool and fish restaurants.
★ **Ponta do Pargo:** the most westerly point; wild and desolate.

Opposite: *Ponta do Pargo, the most westerly point of the island.*

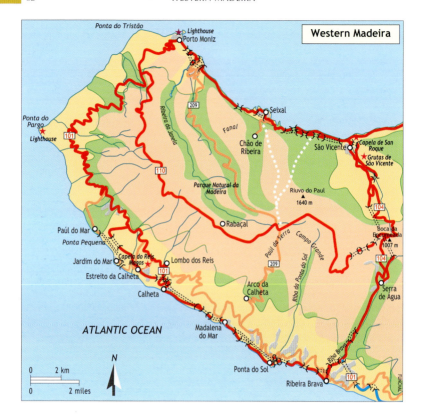

PONTA DO PARGO ★

Ponta do Pargo means 'Dolphin Point', a reference to the dolphin-fish (*pargos*) still caught in local waters. There's not much to see in this remote village but if you're looking for peace and quiet, you've come to the right place – contact the tourist offices in Funchal or Porto Moniz for information about bungalows and holiday lets in the vicinity. Once a year, on or around the third weekend in September, the village puts on its glad rags for the **Apple Festival** (it's said that sailors can detect the aroma far out at sea). Ponta do Pargo is the most westerly point of the island – next stop, America. As you leave the village, look for the turning to the **lighthouse** (*farol*) and follow the signs

Opposite: *The lighthouse at Ponta do Pargo.*

for about 3km (2 miles) along the track. The outlook to sea from the clifs is well worth the detour.

There's a popular coastal walk following the *levada* from **Ponta do Pargo** to **Calheta**, with uninterrupted views of the Atlantic Ocean on one side and the ridges of the **Paúl da Serra** on the other. You'll need to bring sunglasses and sunblock as the path is south-facing with only occasional shade from pine and eucalyptus.

PONTA DO SOL

In days gone by, African slaves worked the sugar plantations around Ponta do Sol, inspiring the 'carriers' dance, patterned on the movements of labourers jogging to and from the mills, laden with heavy baskets. The most prominent slave owner was the Flemish sugar merchant and friend of Columbus, Jeannin Esmerandt (João Esmeraldo) who built a country estate for himself here; it still survives, though in a much-altered form. The parish church is dedicated to **Our Lady of Light** (Nossa Senhora da Luz) – a pointer, perhaps, to the town's reputation for basking in year-round sunlight. The wooden *Mudéjar* ceiling dates from the time of King Manuel I, as does the green ceramic font and the exquisite *azulejos* (hand-decorated tiles). Follow the cobbled streets down to the beach where you can pick your way across the pebbles for a cooling dip. Or take a stroll along the promenade or explore the new **Marina de Lugar de Baixo**, where you'll find yachts, shops, restaurants, a gym, swimming pools and a lagoon with an exhibition on ecotourism; tel: 291 970 160.

DIVING WRECK

Several diving schools visit the wreck of the *Bowbelle*, 25m (82ft) beneath the waves off **Ponta do Sol**. The boat has a tragic history. On 20 August 1989 the *Bowbelle*, a gravel dredger on London's River Thames, was involved in a collision with a pleasure cruiser, the *Marchioness*, resulting in the death of 51 of the 131 people on board, mostly young people attending a party. Several years later, the *Bowbelle* was sold to a Madeiran company where it was registered under a new name, the *Bom Rei*. In March 1996 the *Bom Rei* broke in two and sank during a storm, one crew member losing his life in the incident.

ROOTS

Though the celebrated American author, John Dos Passos (1896–1970), was born in Chicago, his grandparents came from **Ponta do Sol**. Dos Passos deals almost exclusively with urban and industrial themes in novels like *Manhattan Transfer* (1925) and the *USA* trilogy (1930–38). Perhaps it was a lingering affinity for his ancestral home that induced him to pay Ponta do Sol a brief visit when he was already in his sixties – a plaque on the wall of the town hall recalls the occasion. Having paid his respects, he returned to his suite in Reid's Hotel.

HENRIQUE ALEMÃO

'Henry the German' was, in fact, King Wladislaw III of Poland, who gave up his throne after suffering a crushing defeat at the Battle of Varna in 1414. His plans to make a round-the-world pilgrimage were scuppered when he was shipwrecked off the coast of Madeira, but his fortunes improved after **Zarco** made him a gift of land near **Madalena do Mar**. It turned out that Wladislaw was a born farmer, and the local community prospered as a result. Wladislaw married the daughter of a Portuguese nobleman but died tragically when a landslide off **Cabo Girão** destroyed his ship as he was about to set out on a journey to Portugal. We know what he looked like because he appears in the painting, *Santa Ana and São Joaquim*, in the **Museu de Arte Sacra**.

THE WEST COAST

The stretch of coastline between Ponta do Sol and Ponta do Pargo makes a rewarding drive which you could complete in a morning or afternoon, even with detours.

The parish of **Madalena do Mar** was founded in 1457 by the enigmatic Henrique Alemão (*see panel, this page*), who is buried in the church. The village is little more than a ribbon of houses strung along the seafront. There's usually plenty of room on the long strip of pebbly sand, where you'll find cafés, shower facilities and, likely as not, volleyball enthusiasts. Just past the village there's a side turning which winds tortuously in the direction of **Arco da Calheta**, from where there are good coastal views.

In **Calheta** itself, the main draw, apart from the imported golden sand beaches, is the **Centro de Artes das Mudas**. The Casa das Mudas was owned by a grandson of Zarco and is now an integral part of the cultural centre. Apart from enjoying first-class art exhibitions, visitors can feast their eyes on the views and enjoy the architecture – the centre was nominated for a Mies Van der Rohe award in 2005. It is open Tuesday–Sunday 10:00–19:00. **Calheta Marina** (Porto de Recreio da Calheta, tel: 291 822 808) is a Mecca for water-sports enthusiasts, but there are opportunities for pleasure boating, yachting, shopping and picnicking too.

There are three interesting churches in the area. The *alfarge* geometrical patterning on the ceiling of **Calheta parish church** has survived intact – only Funchal Cathedral has a finer example. Equally noteworthy is the beautiful silver and ebony tabernacle in the sanctuary. **Arco da Calheta church** dates from the 18th century, but some of the original Manueline features can still be seen – the south portal, the font and the *Mudéjar* roof, since overpainted. The **Chapel of the Three Kings** at **Lombo dos Reis** (near Estreito de Calheta) is worth a detour for the sumptuous 16th-century oak altarpiece depicting the journey of the magi, commissioned from Antwerp's finest craftsmen. From Estreito da Calheta, take the turning to **Jardim do Mar** (literally 'garden of the sea'). This picture-postcard pretty fishing village hosted the World Surfing Championships in January 2001, drawing competitors from as far afield as Brazil and Australia. Here and in the neighbouring villages of **Paúl do Mar** and **Ponta Pequena**, Atlantic rollers of awesome dimensions – 5m (16ft) plus – break over the black basalt shingle. Ride these waves if you dare! They are not for the inexperienced.

Water-sports enthusiasts should also check out the **Calheta Beach Hotel**, about 10 minutes from the village.

Above: *The painted ceiling in the parish church of Arco da Calheta.*
Opposite: *Volleyball players making the most of the evening sunshine on Calheta beach.*

Right: *A statue of Zarco, erected to commemorate the 500th anniversary of the discovery of Madeira.*
Opposite: *The splendid Church of São Bento in Ribeira Brava boasts a number of original Manueline features.*

> ### MANUELINE ARCHITECTURE
>
> During the reign of Manuel I (1495–1521) Portugal gave birth to its own, distinctive architectural style, inspired by the voyages of discovery and funded by the vast wealth pouring into the country from the New World. The most distinctive aspect of the Manueline style is the embellishment of doorways, arches, window frames and capitals, often with nautical motifs. Examples on Madeira include **Funchal Cathedral**, the **Church of the Incarnation**, Funchal, the Church of **São Bento** in Ribeira Brava (font and pulpit), the parish church at **Santa Cruz** (portals), and **Quinta das Cruzes** (window frames preserved in the garden).

RIBEIRA BRAVA

Thanks to the new expressway this small, touristy resort fringed with banana plantations is a mere 15 minutes away by car from Funchal. If you have the time though, it's worth considering the boat excursion which makes a stop here via **Câmara de Lobos** and the spectacular cliffs at **Cabo Girão**.

The name 'Ribeira Brava' means 'wild river'. If you're here in July and August when the river bed is covered with vegetation, even the notion of a torrent is inconceivable. Yet it's a fact that, over time measured in millennia, the huge ravine running parallel with the road to São Vicente is the work of this fitfully mighty waterway.

The one tourist sight is the **Church of São Bento** (St Benedict). The Baroque bell tower with its overlarge clock, checkerboard steeple and decorative balusters has a slightly surreal aspect, though it was founded in the 15th century. Things to look out for in the cool, pristine interior include the original Manueline arches, the carvings on the 16th-century font (near the entrance), and the pulpit, ornamented with sailors' knot motifs.

Ribeira Brava is a good place to shop for gifts: not just the predictable mugs and T-shirts but wooden toboggans and caravels, glassware, wickerwork, embroidered place mats, tablecloths, etc. The **old harbour** lies through a tunnel in the rock, but a new, sheltered area is available to tourists along the main seafront.

Ribeira Brava's red-letter day is the feast of St Peter (29 June), when garlands of paper flowers are strung across the cobbled streets and revellers from across the island arrive by boat to cook barbecues of skewered beef (*espetada*) on the stony beach.

Porto Moniz ★

A small seaside resort 75km (47 miles) northwest of Funchal, Porto Moniz is one of the remotest points on the island but it's also one of the busiest, at least at lunchtimes when coach parties descend on the hotel complex behind the promenade. The seafood restaurants are the main draw here – you'll need to book ahead or come early to be sure

ETHNOGRAPHICAL MUSEUM

The **Museu Etnográfico da Madeira** in Ribeira Brava offers a fascinating insight into the history of the island's trades and handicrafts including weaving, farming, viticulture and fishing. Local craftsmen give demonstrations. The 16th-century building was formerly a rum distillery and sugar cane mill and you can still see some of the original equipment, notably the water wheel. There is a café on the premises and a shop selling souvenirs. Rua de São Francisco 24, tel: 291 952 598. Open Tuesday–Sunday 10:00–12:30, 14:00–18:00, closed on holidays.

SCIENCE BY THE SEA

The Living Science Centre is funded by the regional government with the goal of promoting science, especially among young people. The large museum space stages exhibitions on a wide range of subjects, from communicating via the five senses, to astronomy, medicine and the science of sport. The emphasis throughout is on interaction – even the play area is designated a 'cyber zone' and is equipped with internet.
Centro de Ciencia Viva, Porto Moniz, tel: 291 850 300, website: www.ccvportomoniz.com Open Tuesday–Sunday 10:00–19:00.

of a table. It's a short, but bracing stroll from the bus stop (last service to São Vicente, 14:30) along the seafront, via the tourist office and the excellent gift shop, Bordarte Souvenirs, where you can buy everything from ornamental banana trees to anthologies of Madeiran folk music. These 'Songs of the Sea', with their tales of hazard and shipwreck, were inspired by the treacherous coastline – the volcanic rocks, like the armour-plated backs of stegosauruses, seem to lurk in the spume. The salt spray permeates the air and is a potential danger to the crops growing on the hillsides. The best defence, local farmers have found, is to build screens of heather, bracken, brushwood or whatever else comes to hand.

Porto Moniz boasts one of the most attractive **lidos** on the island, its natural lava pools connected by a series of concrete bridges and walkways. After a dip, take the new cable car linking the beach with **Achadas da Cruz** (open daily 10:00–18:00) or visit the **Living Science Centre** (see panel, this page).

Seixal

If you've come to Madeira to relax, this sleepy, unselfconscious hamlet – call it a village at a push – is just the place. It's also an ideal base for exploring the rugged north coast and the enchanting hinterland around Fanal. Seixal makes its living not from fishing, as you might first suspect, but from agriculture. The local grape, Sercial, produces the

Below: *The view from one of the numerous* miradouros *on the winding road leading down to Porto Moniz.*

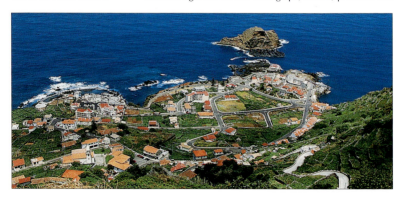

Above: *Porto Moniz's natural rock pools have been transformed into a splendid lido.*

driest of Madeiran wines, and is grown on the precipitous slopes to the rear of the village. If you've a head for heights, take a closer look at the vines, trained over raised trestles to protect them from the fungal diseases that thrive on damp soil. Subtropical fruits, including mangoes, avocados, figs and sugar apples, all flourish in the fertile Seixal valley.

The village offers little to tourists but itself. As the twisting lanes and passageways drop towards the sea, most of them turn out to be cul-de-sacs, an invitation to linger and enjoy the charm of the houses, decorated with *azulejo* shrines to the Virgin or St Vincent, and brightly painted chimneys that resemble miniature campaniles.

From the quay an unusual rock formation reaches into the sea like an outstretched hand. Steps lead down to the water but the fishermen won't thank you for spoiling their sport; in any case, swimming is not recommended – huge ray fish have been spotted only a few metres from the shore and currents are strong and unpredictable. The rock pool *piscina* nearby is fed directly by the sea, which swells and foams ominously near the stepladders at high tide. The pick of Seixal's restaurants is **O Aquario** where, as the name suggests, octopus and other seafood feature prominently on the menu.

Sugar Mill

Sugar production in the Calheta region began back in the 15th century, though there are few signs of it today. However, the **Engenho da Calheta** is an early 20th-century mill which distills sugar into rum. You can sample the product after exploring the distillery at your leisure. The mill is located next to the Igreja Matriz (Parish Church), tel: 291 822 264. Open Monday–Friday 08:00–19:00.

WINE GROWING

The wine harvest begins in August with the picking of the Malvasia and Bual grapes that mature earlier than the Sercial and Verdelho varieties. The vines are cultivated on *poios*, narrow step-like terraces carved out of the hillside. To prevent devastation from mildew and other fungal blights, they are trained on trellises, raising them above ground level. After Oidium and then *Phylloxera* had almost wiped out the industry in the mid-19th century, growers turned to the Tinta Negra Mole grape that is still used to produce younger, less exclusive wines, the traditional varieties being in relatively short supply.

Blue and pink acanthus brighten the road to **Chão de Ribeira**, an EU-funded agricultural development about 3km (2 miles) above the village. Women in headscarves, carrying cabbages and potatoes from the market gardens, will greet you along the way. The restaurant at Chão has unpredictable opening times so if you're planning on lunch, pack a picnic – there are tables waiting for you.

FANAL

One of Madeira's unsung beauty spots, Fanal could be an enjoyable half-day excursion from Porto Moniz or Seixal. Since 1982 this thickly wooded mountain ridge, more than 1000m (3280ft) above sea level, has been administered by the National Park of Madeira which conserves the endemic flora and fauna, including endangered species like the *Freira da Madeira* (laurel pigeon). To get to Fanal take the EN209 from Porto Moniz, but check your suspension beforehand as this 'road' is little more than a track in places. Leave the car near the Forestry Station and relish the stark grandeur of a landscape untamed and unaltered in a thousand years. If you'd rather not make the trip on your own (mists descend regularly), Madeira Trails of Adventure (see www.madeira-island.com/aventura) organize jeep safaris to Fanal, stopping en route to see the volcanic crater.

THE NORTH COAST ROAD

The 19km (12-mile) stretch of road from São Vicente to Porto Moniz makes an exhilarating, if demanding, drive (allow between 45 minutes and one hour). Period photographs document the formidable obstacles that had to be overcome in the building of this highway. It took men with an enviable head for heights and the agility of mountain goats more than 16 years to carve the cliff tunnels from the bare rock.

Before you set out, bear in mind the rules of the road here – give way to oncoming traffic at all times and remember to drive slowly, as there's an unnerving number of hairpin bends ahead. Sea spray from the pounding Atlantic breakers and the cascades from the cliff face, which land indiscriminately on any vehicle in their path, are some of the hazards you'll have to face. Be as phlegmatic about the latter as the locals, who think of it as a free car wash!

QUINTAS

Most of the survivng *quintas* (out-of-town estates) date from the late 17th century onwards and were built by prominent local families, or foreign (mainly British) settlers. Many were highly productive agricultural estates with vineyards, orchards and vegetable gardens. During the 19th and early 20th centuries many *quintas* were rented out as holiday homes to foreign royals and other members of the glitterati. While **Quinta das Cruzes** is the only villa open to the public, many of the gardens may be visited: **Quinta Magnólia**, **Quinta do Palheiro Ferreiro**, **Quinta Monte Palace** and **Quinta Vigia** (now part of the **Santa Catarina Gardens**).

Opposite: *The rugged shoreline at São Vicente, typical of Madeira's north coast.*
Left: *Cliff tunnels like this one, on the North Coast Road, were hewn from the rock by hand.*

> **TOP WINE-PRODUCING AREAS**
>
> **Câmara de Lobos:**
> 22,867 hectolitres
> (4,024,592 pints)
> **São Vicente:**
> 20,127 hectolitres
> (3,542,352 pints)
> **Santana:**
> 8039 hectolitres
> (1,414,864 pints)
> **Porto Moniz:**
> 5554 hectolitres
> (977,504 pints)
> **Funchal:**
> 1154 hectolitres
> (203,104 pints)
> **Calheta:**
> 782 hectolitres
> (137,632 pints)
> Figures from *Madeira* by
> Alex Liddell (Faber, 1998).
> For more detailed information
> on Madeiran wines, visit
> www.madeirawineguide.com

SÃO VICENTE

This attractive village lies at the foot of a spectacular, steep-sided valley. If you're approaching from the coast road you'll notice a tiny chapel emerging from a single block of basalt at the mouth of the river. The **Capela de San Roque** was built in 1694 and marks the spot where St Vincent is said to have made a miraculous appearance. Bleak and windswept, the beach is stony and ill-suited to swimming, though the **hotel restaurants** at the far end are worth investigating if you're on the lookout for an evening meal. The core of the village is a little way inland (just follow the course of the river). Palm trees peer down on a 17th-century **parish church** dedicated to St Vincent. The interior is the usual Baroque confection, gaudily painted and with lashings of scrolled gold leaf for decorative effect. There's little to shatter the peace and quiet here – the bandstand on the forecourt is usually empty. Occasionally, however, people do emerge from behind the dazzling, green-shuttered houses to do the shopping or tend the tubs of flowers and potted plants that add a dash of colour to the cobbled lanes.

There's a supermarket if you need to stock up on essentials, as well as a selection of cafés and small restaurants.

Right: *Grapes from São Vicente, now the second largest wine-producing area on the island.*

Left: *Getting about Madeira can be a time-consuming business as there are many natural barriers to negotiate.*

It's a 15-minute walk from the village to the **Grutas de São Vicente**. This cave system was formed some 400,000 years ago when the **volcanoes** of the Paúl da Serra erupted, spewing streams of molten lava down the mountainside, hollowing out the melting rock in the process. The galleries were discovered by an English visitor in 1855. They extend for more than 700m (2297ft), although only about 70m (230ft) is open to the public (allow about half an hour for a guided tour) from 10:00–19:00 daily; tel: 291 842 404.

Inside, the temperature is constant. Plant seeds carried in by water seeping through the rock grow only because of the presence of artificial light. These caves too have stalactites, only here they never grow – they were formed in an instant when the drops of molten rock froze on the spot. You can learn more about the caves in the **Volcano Pavilion and Water Gardens**.

Paúl da Serra

Bleak, inhospitable yet strangely beautiful, Paúl da Serra is a windswept moorland plateau 1200–1500m (3940–4920ft) above sea level. Sheep, goats and cattle

AZULEJOS

Whether it's a church, a drinking fountain, a market hall, a car showroom or a private house you're looking at, the chances are that *azulejos* will feature in the decoration. The art of glazing and hand-painting tiles is a legacy of the Moorish converts to Christianity who lived in southern Portugal during the Middle Ages. At first the designs were exclusively geometrical, in line with the teaching of the *Koran* which forbids the depiction of the human or animal form in art. Figurative subjects start appearing later in the 17th century, about the same time as yellows and greens drop from the colour scheme in favour of the now familiar blue-on-white.

graze among the clumps of ferns and heather but, save for an idiosyncratic hotel and café, there are few signs of human habitation. It's usually freezing cold up here – if you intend getting out of the car, take a jumper. Before you set out, check on the weather – you'll see little or nothing when the mist descends and the shepherds take shelter in mountain caves. If you have the right equipment (hiking boots, warm clothing, an anorak, and water) and want to make the trip from Funchal, take a taxi to the **statue of Cristo Rei** (Christ the King) on the edge of the Campo Grande then follow the *levada* channel. It's an exhilarating feeling skirting the plateau, volcanic peaks in one direction and a panoramic sweep of the coastal fishing villages of Madalena do Mar, Calheta, Ponta do Sol, etc., in the other.

RABAÇAL ★★★

Flanked by the peaks of the Paúl da Serra, the luxuriant scenery of the Rabaçal valley has always enchanted visitors. The location is a special favourite with hikers, as not one but three *levadas* converge to feed the hydroelectric power station at Calheta. Rabaçal is accessible only by car so if you don't want to bring your own vehicle, hire a taxi for the day – it's worth it. The starting point for walks is on the main road, from where a minor road (not open to cars) leads down to the government forestry station where the amenities include toilets, barbecue stands and picnic tables. For a gentle stroll, follow the **Levada do Risco** from the forestry station for 15 minutes and you'll arrive at the falls, a spectacular cataract which plunges 100m (330ft) over a sheer cliff into the ravine below. The local humidity accounts for the ragged curtain of lichen clinging to the rock. The **Levada dos 25 Fontes** leads to another beauty spot – a small clearing in the primeval laurel forest where ribbons of water seep from hidden clefts in the rock, before tumbling into an emerald pool. (Allow about an hour for the round trip.) If you have extra reserves of energy, double back and take the turn-off to the **Levada do Rocha Vermelha** which traverses the lower reaches of the Rabaçal gorge en route to the valley of the Ribeira de Janela. Here you'll encounter beauty of a different kind as you leave the laurel forest behind for a more open landscape of grassy hillsides and heath trees.

> **TAKE A PICNIC**
>
> There are few more enjoyable places for picnicking than Madeira with its spectacular scenery. Some choice spots are the Bica da Cana observation point in the **Paúl da Serra**, the government rest house at **Rabaçal** (also in the Paúl da Serra), the woods at **Ribeiro Frio**, and the Queimadas rest house at the beginning of the *levada* walk to **Caldeirão Verde**.

Opposite: *The hillside village of São Vicente is sheltered from coastal winds.*
Below: *Typically rugged terrain in the Paúl da Serra – desolate, all but uninhabited and frequently shrouded in mist.*

WALKERS' GUIDEBOOKS

Pat and John Underwood's *Landscapes of Madeira* first appeared in 1980 and is still an invaluable guide to *levada* walking on the island, with incredibly detailed maps, route marches and practical advice. You'll find it on sale in bookshops in Funchal; alternatively visit the website: www.sunflowerbooks.co.uk
A much more recent and comprehensive guide is Paddy Dillon's *Walking in Madeira*, published by Cicerone. *See* www.cicerone.co.uk

BOCA DA ENCUMEADA ***

Midway along the north-south highway connecting **Ribeira Brava** with **Sâo Vicente** is the **Encumeada Pass**, one of the best-known *miradouros* (lookouts) on the island. The vantage point is 1004m (3294ft) high but what you see from here depends very much on the weather – whorls of cloud may obscure the view below even as you enjoy bright sunlight on the ledge. On the other hand, strike it lucky and much of the northern coastline unfolds in one direction, and the Serra de Agua in the other. There's a small café with picnic tables near the car park, but if you've brought lunch with you there are choicer spots in the woods. Keep the camera handy because there are more *miradouros* as the road descends south to the Pousada dos Vinháticos Hotel – make a reservation to be sure of a table with a view in the Restaurant Pousada. Cosily ensconced in the valley below is the village of **Serra de Água**, literally 'sawmill', where there are several small hotels and bungalows, should you wish to stay overnight. If you're feeling energetic, there's a great walk from Encumeada to **Boca da Corrida** with rewarding views of **Curral das Freiras** and several mountain peaks, including **Pico Grande** and **Pico de Serradinho**. Only moderately difficult, it will take you about 3½ hours to complete.

Below: *The river valley of Serra de Água is a majestic sight.*

Western Madeira at a Glance

Best Times to Visit

July–September are best for festivals: '**Week by the Sea**', Porto Moniz, first week August. **Grape harvest**, villages along north and west coast, first two weeks September. **Apple festival**, Ponta do Pargo, usually third weekend September. **Council week** (gastronomy), Câmara de Lobos, first week July.

Getting There

Buses leave Rodoeste bus station on Rua Ribeira João Gomes, Funchal, for Ribeira Brava, São Vicente, Seixal, Porto Moniz, Boca de Encumeada, Ponta do Pargo, Ponta do Sol and Calheta. The **expressway** from Funchal is the quickest way of reaching Ribeira Brava by car (15 min); **boat excursions** from Funchal marina also stop here.

Getting Around

Hire a car or taxi. Bus services are infrequent. In Porto Moniz the private cabs in the main square tend to overcharge.

Where to Stay

Hotel Baia do Sol, Rua Doctor João Augusto Teixeira, Ponto do Sol, tel: 291 970 140, website: www.enotel.com Elegant seaside hotel, 71 rooms, some with balconies and sea views. Restaurant, indoor pool and small fitness room.
Country House Atrio, Lombo dos Moinhos Acima, Estreito da Calheta, tel: 291 820 400, fax: 291 820 419, website: www.atrio-madeira.com Ten rooms, all with sea and garden views, some with balconies. Restaurant, heated outdoor pool.
Hotel Jardim do Mar, Sítio da Piedade, Jardim do Mar, tel: 291 823 616, fax: 291 823 617. Pleasant; in one of the loveliest villages on the island.
Pensão Brisa Mar, Sítio do Cais, Seixal, tel: 291 854 476, fax: 291 854 477. Family-run hotel with excellent sea views.
Estalagem do Vale, Sitio da Feiteira de Baixo, São Vicente 9240-206, tel: 291 840 160, website: www.estalagemdovale.com Tastefully converted 18th-century manor house.
Pensão Praia Mar, Sítio do Calhau, São Vicente, tel: 291 842 383, fax: 291 842 749. Small, but attractive seafront hotel with comfortable rooms.
Pousada dos Vinháticos, Serra de Agua 9350-306, tel: 291 775 936, website: www.pousadadosvinhaticos.com Small guesthouse; basic facilities.

Where to Eat

Onda Azul, Hotel Calheta Beach, Vila da Calheta, tel: 291 820 313. Discerning locals patronize this restaurant where grilled fish is the speciality. Save room for mouthwatering desserts.
Casa de Pasto, Sítio Chão da Ribeira, Seixal, tel: 291 854 559. Feast on grilled *espetada* and other fine examples of Madeiran home cooking, while enjoying the views at this famous beauty spot.
Restaurant Pousada, Pousada dos Vinháticos (*see above*), tel: 291 952 344. Hotel restaurant specializing in homely cooking such as soups, and meat dishes like *espetada*.

Tours and Excursions

Madeira Explorers & Heliatlantis, *see page 59*.
NATURA, Actividades Turisticas, Box 4072, Funchal, tel: 291 236 015, fax: 291 238 652. Organizes walking tours.
Madeira Airbase Airadventures, Sítio das Achadas de Santo Antão 9370-011, Arco da Calheta, tel (mobile): 964 133 907, website: www.madeira-paragliding.com
Diving: Clube Naval do Seixal Cais do Seixal, Porto Moniz, tel: 965 013 572.

Useful Contacts

Tourist Offices:
Ponta do Sol, Centro de Observação de Natureza, tel: 291 972 850. Open Monday–Friday 09:00–12:30, 14:00–17:00, Saturday 09:00–12:00;
Ribeira Brava, Forte de São Bento, tel: 291 951 675. Open Monday–Friday 09:00–12:30, 14:00–17:00, Saturday 09:30–12:00;
Porto Moniz, Vila do Porto Moniz, tel: 291 852 555. Open Monday–Friday 10:00–15:00, Saturday 12:00–15:00.
Marina do Lugar de Baixo, Ponta do Sol, tel: 291 970 160, fax: 291 970 169. Water sports, yacht moorings, gym, pools, lagoon, restaurants.
Porto de Recreo da Calheta, tel: 291 824 003, fax: 291 824 006. Yachting and shopping.

4
Central Madeira

It is said that when Queen Isabella of Spain asked Columbus to describe one of her new island possessions, he replied by taking a piece of paper and crumpling it in his hands. The story probably relates to Jamaica but could equally well apply to the landscape of central Madeira, its chain of volcanic peaks forming a stupendous natural barrier between the northern and southern parts of the island. Reaching them is relatively straightforward, though the road from Funchal is among the most tortuous on the island. Beyond the genteel suburb of **Monte**, with its famous twin-towered church and Tropical Garden, lies the Poiso pass and the turn-off to Madeira's third highest mountain, **Pico do Arieiro**. The views from the summit (accessible by car) are a highlight of any visit. There are more views to the west, from the *miradouro* overlooking the hidden valley of **Curral das Freiras** – 'one of the great sights of the world' according to H N Coleridge, nephew of the great English poet. To the east, a tract of tangled laurel forest leads to **Ribeiro Frio** ('cold stream') where hikers pick up the Levada do Furado for Balcões. From this vantage point – Balcões means 'balconies' – one can enjoy vistas of the Ribeira da Metade valley, Faial (a *miradouro* in its own right) and the northern coast.

The coastal road from Faial to Ponta Delgada is tortuous but picturesque, skirting ravines and rounding the heads of river valleys like the spectacular **Ribeira do Pôrco** at Boaventura. Each turn in the road offers a new perspective on the scattered hamlets, littering the hillsides like broken fragments of china on a baize cloth. The

Don't Miss

★★★ **Monte:** Tropical Garden, Church of Our Lady of Monte, and toboggan rides.
★★★ **Curral das Freiras:** views of the 'hidden valley'.
★★ **Câmara de Lobos:** fishing village painted by Sir Winston Churchill.
★★ ***Levada* walks:** Ribeiro Frio and Pico das Pedras National Park.
★★ **Cabo Girão:** world's second highest cliff.

Opposite: *The Church of Our Lady of Monte, an important centre of pilgrimage.*

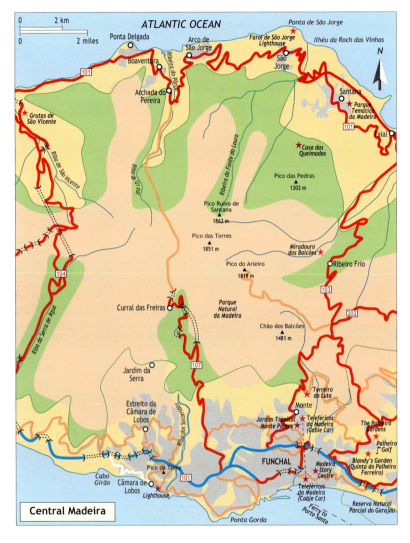

largest of these, **Santana**, features on every tourist itinerary but it's the walks in the **Pico das Pedras National Park**, rather than the celebrated thatched cottages, that linger in the memory.

CÂMARA DE LOBOS ★★

This famously picturesque fishing village is only 5km (3 miles) from Funchal and makes a great lunch stop. The name means 'sea wolf's lair', an allusion to the seals spotted by Zarco off the coast centuries ago. Life still revolves around the pebble beach and the adjoining boatyard, where the leathery-faced fishermen mend their nets or add an extra coat to their garishly painted boats. It's all very photogenic from the tourist's point of view but the reality is that most seamen barely make a living and are usually confined to port. At a loose end, they pass the time playing dominoes and enjoying a few glasses of *ponchas*, the local tipple made from lemon juice, honey and rum. Leave *ponchas* at least until you've had a chance to feast on grilled *espada* (scabbard fish), the speciality of the homely restaurants off the main square. *Espada* is just one of the gastronomic treats in store if you happen upon Câmara during 'Council Week' (after 29 June).

Below: *The picturesque fishing village of Câmara de Lobos.*

Going Up

Visitors can enjoy spectacular views of the cliffs between Câmara de Lobos and Cabo Girão by taking the **Caldeira de Rancho cable car**. Designed initially with farmers in mind, the service operates between Rancho, where there's a restaurant and snack bar serving *espada* and other traditional Madeiran dishes, and the (stony) beach at Fajãs do Cabo Girão.
Rancho cable car, Estrada de Santa Clara/Rancho de Cima, open Sunday 09:00–19:00, Monday 08:00–09:00 and 17:00–20:00, and Tuesday–Friday 08:00–19:00.

Beyond the boatyard some steps lead to the terrace where Sir Winston Churchill sought painterly inspiration. It took only one well-documented visit by the great statesman, in January 1950, to put Câmara de Lobos on the map.

Historians still dispute whether the **Capela de Nossa Senhora da Conceição** predates the chapel at Machico (both date from around 1420, making them the oldest extant religious foundations on the island). One of the primitive wall paintings in the former depicts St Nicholas delivering hard-bitten sailors from shipwreck off the Lycian coast. The parish church of **St Sebastian** is a little further up the hill and worth a quick look for the *talha dourada* (gilded wood) altarpiece, a fine example of Portuguese Baroque.

It's only a short drive from Câmara de Lobos to the *miradouro* at **Pico das Torres** (panoramic views all the way from Funchal Bay to Cabo Girão). Follow the climbing road for just a few more kilometres and you'll reach **Estreito da Câmara de Lobos**, known for its cherries and sugar cane, but more important as a wine-growing centre. At harvest time (on or around the second week in September) there's a **festival** devoted to viticulture, with demonstrations, tastings, etc. If the mood takes you, you could make a short detour

Right: *The Capela de Nossa Senhora da Conceição in Câmara de Lobos, founded early in the 15th century.*

Above: Houses cling precariously to the cliffs beneath Cabo Girão.

from Estreito to the scenic hamlet of **Jardim da Serra** where the celebrated 19th-century diplomat, Henry Veitch, built a *quinta* (closed to the public).

Cabo Girão ★★

You can reach this justly celebrated viewing point by road from Funchal in about 45 minutes. At 580m (1900ft), Cabo Girão is the world's fourth highest cliff (Norway holds the number one spot). Vertigo-inducing sea birds circle and swoop around the summit, as if daring you to follow them to the treacherous rocks below. Spare a thought for the ill-fated Henrique Alemão, whose ship came to grief there more than 500 years ago (see panel, page 64). Spare a thought too for the poor Madeiran farmer who has to scramble down the crumbling paths to cultivate the threadbare scraps of terrace carved from the cliff face. There's not much to keep you at the Cape apart from the souvenir stalls, the café and a small exhibition of old photographs. If you arrive reasonably early, you could take the path near the car park and walk to the attractive fishing village of **Câmara de Lobos**, arriving in time for lunch (allow about two hours). The descent is relatively easy, even for the vertically challenged, and you'll be

Bird's-eye View

Heliatlantis offers helicopter trips over Madeira – an expensive but unforgettable way of seeing the island. There are several routes to choose from:
• A 10-minute sweep of **Funchal Bay**.
• A 15-minute overview of **Curral das Freiras**.
• A 30-minute round-trip to the east or west of the island.
• A 45-minute tour of the entire island.
Each helicopter can take up to five people at a time (prices quoted are per person).

Above: *The spectacular view of Curral das Freiras from the* miradouro *at Eagle's Nest.*
Opposite: *Local handicrafts are on sale all over the island, as here at Monte.*

rewarded with views of Funchal Bay, as far as the Islas Desertas if the weather is favourable. You could pass the time trying to identify the astonishing variety of crops growing on the hillsides – everything from strawberries to potatoes.

CURRAL DAS FREIRAS ★★★

About 15km (9.3 miles) northwest of Funchal (allow at least 45 minutes if driving), this spectacular valley, enclosed by gaunt mountain peaks, is one of the island's top attractions and a 'must see'. The name Curral das Freiras means 'corral or enclosure for nuns' and dates from 1497 when João Gonçalves da Câmara gave the Santa Clara Convent sole pasture rights as an endowment – two of his daughters were novices. According to tradition, the nuns of Santa Clara took refuge here when French corsairs sacked Funchal in 1566 – the reason for the more usual translation of 'refuge' or 'hideaway'. For photographs the best vantage point is the *miradouro* at **Eira do Serrado**, about 450m (1476ft) above the village – at the roadside you'll see locals picking eucalyptus leaves to scent their cars. Foreign visitors have marvelled at the views since at least the 1820s when the usual mode of transport was the hammock (*see* panel, page 85). It was long believed that the valley was the crater of a long extinct volcano. Today most geologists favour erosion as the most likely explanation but the issue is still hotly debated. Less than 50 years ago the only way down to the village was the snaking path that starts beyond the souvenir stalls near the road tunnel. It takes a little over an hour to walk to the church from the

CURRAL DAS FREIRAS AND MONTE

miradouro and the scenery along the way is breathtaking. Curral das Freiras itself heaves with visitors, especially on Sunday (market day) when it's as brash and unsentimental as a frontier town during the gold rush. It's famous for its chestnuts – chestnut cakes, chestnut soups, even chestnut liqueur (*licor de castanha*) – and there's a **chestnut festival** in November. Souvenirs tend to be overpriced – household items like oven gloves, embroidered tea towels and slippers seem better value. Before you move on, take a peek at the church (no sign of nuns here nowadays) and the tiny cemetery, where photographs of the deceased adorn the tombstones.

MONTE ★★★

Reaching Funchal's genteel garden suburb couldn't be easier. Eight-seater **cable-car** cabins take just 11 minutes to cover the 6km (3.7-mile) journey and the views of the bay on the ascent are stunning. Monte's heyday as a fashionable resort was at the end of the 19th century, when the Palace Hotel ran a sanatorium for the wealthy sufferers of tuberculosis. It's now a private home but the grounds are open to the public as a small museum and the **Tropical Garden** (Caminho do Monte), a 7ha (17-acre)

> **ISLAND TRAVEL**
>
> Madeirans have been ingenious in devising modes of transport specially suited to the mountainous terrain. Until the early 20th century, visitors were ferried in hammocks slung on poles and carried by two strapping men. The young Winston Churchill was fascinated by the *carro de bois*, a sledge with wooden runners, pulled by a pair of bullocks in harness (useful for negotiating Funchal's steep, cobbled streets). The Monte **toboggan** (*carro de cesto*) is still in service after nearly 150 years, though only as a tourist attraction. The **rack-and-pinion railway** that once connected Funchal with Terreiro da Luta was closed in 1939 after an engine exploded, killing four people.

Last Emperor

Karl I von Habsburg was deposed as Emperor of Austria-Hungary in November 1918, after reigning for barely two years. He and his wife chose Madeira as their place of exile after first settling in Switzerland. They were given a warm reception when they arrived in Funchal harbour, on-board a British ship, in November 1921. Shortly afterwards they moved from Reid's Hotel to the **Quinta do Monte** which had been placed at their disposal by the owner, a Portuguese aristocrat. Karl died in April 1922, aged 35, after succumbing to a bout of pneumonia. Many Roman Catholics came to regard him as a saint and his canonization was formally proposed in 1949.

horticultural theme park with more than 100,000 plants from around the world, including 60 varieties of cycad. This ancient fern-like plant probably originated in Egypt but was in this case introduced from South Africa, where the present owner of the estate, José Berardo, made his fortune. Berardo's landscape gardeners were given free rein to create a wonderland of grottoes, spouting fountains, ornamental bridges, pagodas, streams and ponds stocked with Chinese koi fish. The Tropical Garden is open Monday–Friday 09:30–18:00; tel: 291 742 650.

When the spotlights are turned on the twin-towered **Church of Our Lady of Monte**, it becomes a landmark visible from Funchal itself. A chapel was founded on this site by the first Madeirans to be born on the island (appropriately named Adam and Eve). The present building dates from the early 19th century.

Every year on the Feast of the Assumption (15 August) a medieval statue of the Virgin, said to have miraculous powers, becomes a focus for worshippers from around the island. They climb the 74 steps leading to the church on their hands and knees as a mark of devotion. The marble chapel in the grounds is the last resting place of the former

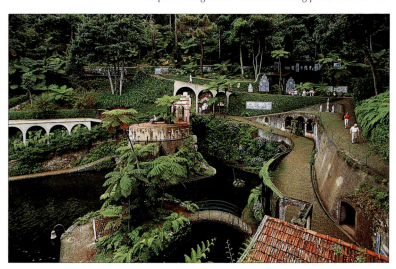

Left: *The Monte toboggan, a mode of transport unique to Madeira.*
Opposite: *The Tropical Garden at Monte was conceived as a flight of fancy.*

emperor of Austria-Hungary, Karl von Habsburg (*see* panel, page 86). The grounds of the **Quinta do Monte** (Jardins do Imperador) are open to the public. From the café in the Malakof Tower there are superb views over Monte towards Funchal.

Today Monte's main claim to fame is the **toboggan** (*carro de cesto*) steered and propelled (where necessary) by able-bodied men of all ages and sizes, kitted out like gondoliers. The bumpy ride down polished roads takes you to Livramento, just halfway to Funchal. Bear in mind, when considering the cost, that you will need to complete your experience by taking a taxi either back up to Monte or down to Funchal.

If you don't want to go directly back to town, take the eucalyptus-lined road up to **Terreiro da Luta**, a noted beauty spot about 300m (984ft) above Monte. The funicular railway that used to run to here was abandoned in the 1930s – the station has been refashioned as a restaurant. After admiring the views, take a look at the monumental **statue of Our Lady of Peace**. It was erected in 1927 at the instigation of a local priest, who had lived through the bombardment of Funchal during World War I – the links

---

LEVADA WALKING

Do's and Don'ts:
• Take some or all of the following: high-factor sun lotion, sunglasses, a hat or cap, a warm jumper, strong, comfortable shoes with a good grip, a rainproof jacket, a pair of woollen socks, a camera, binoculars.
• Never set out without checking the weather and the state of the tracks and mountain passes.
• Never walk alone.
• Take a detailed, up-to-date map with you.
• Bring a torch if there are tunnels to negotiate.
• Have a few written phrases in Portuguese handy in case you have to ask for directions.
• Be realistic: if you suffer from vertigo, bad back etc. avoid walks which are too challenging.
• Start with an easy walk like Balcões or go with a group or tour party.

Right: *Statue of Our Lady of Peace at Terreiro da Luta, a lasting reminder of World War I.*

> ### What to Buy in Madeira
>
> • **Embroidery** (handkerchiefs, table mats and tablecloths).
> • **Tapestry** on canvas (chair covers, wall hangings, and cushions).
> • **Wickerwork** (hampers, newspaper racks and laundry baskets).
> • **Wine** (the shop in Adegas de São Francisco is the best place to buy Madeira).
> • Postage **stamps** (*Birds of Madeira* series).
> • **Sweetmeats**, e.g. *bolo de mel* (honey cake).
> • **Flowers and plants** (orchids, strelitzias and anthuriums, *see* panels, pages 8 and 55)
> • **Books** about Madeira (the Patio bookshop and the Madeira Story Centre in Funchal have the best selection).
> • **CDs or tapes** of traditional folk music.
> • **Clothes** (items of folk costume, leather boots or *Barretes de la* – the traditional woollen bobble hat with ear flaps, worn by villagers across the island).
> • **Woodcarvings** (miniature Monte toboggans, sailing boats and banana trees).

in the rosary were forged from the anchor chains of Allied ships. The **violet**, pride of Madeira, flowers around the massive basalt base between May and July.

Ribeiro Frio ★★

Picturesque Ribeiro Frio ('cold stream') is a densely wooded location, popular with hikers and bird-watchers – bring binoculars if you have them. Follow the road to the spring-fed **trout hatchery**, a handy source of supply for the local restaurant. While you contemplate lunch, you can enjoy the informal **Botanical Garden**, planted exclusively with indigenous species like Madeira cedar, lily of the valley, buckthorn, cherry laurel, pride of Madeira and yellow foxglove. The most well-trodden of the many walks in the area follows the **Levada do Furado**, signposted just beyond the restaurant. Cross the road, and it's a 30-minute stroll to the observation point of **Miradouro dos Balcões** ('balconies'). Keen-eyed ornithologists have spotted buzzards, plain swifts, grey wagtails, blackcaps, firecrests and the endemic *Columba trocaz* (long-toed pigeon) in the area, and what you don't see you'll be able to hear. From Balcões there are sweeping views of the **Ribeira da Metade valley** as far as the tooth-like outcrop known as Eagle's Nest (Penha de Águia) and seaward to Porto Sauto. Sir Winston Churchill captured this striking landscape in watercolour on one of his visits in the 1950s.

If you are feeling energetic, take the path in the opposite direction to the water house at **Lamaceiros**, where it joins the smaller **Levada do Portela**. Allow about three hours for this walk. It's not particularly taxing but you'll need shoes with a good grip, as the path is slippery in places and there are small streams to ford. You'll also need a good head for heights rounding the precipitous slopes of **Pico do Suna** and crossing the narrow ledge carved from the rock face at **Cabeço Furado**. Stupendous views open up across the Ribeiro Frio valley towards the jagged crown of **Pico das Torres** in the west and São Roque do Faial and the peninsula of **Porto da Cruz** in the north. Along the way you'll see the remnants of the primitive laurel forest which once covered the island and some of the more than 70 varieties of fern which flourish in the humid microclimate.

> ### KILLER DISEASE
>
> Tuberculosis, or consumption as it was more commonly known before the 20th century, was at one time the single largest cause of death in the western world. Doctors were divided as to the treatment of the dreaded wasting disease but there was general agreement that a warm, dry climate was beneficial. Egypt, the French Riviera and Madeira became the favourite winter destinations of the unfortunate invalids and their companions. Those who could afford to, rented *quintas* for the season until the opening of the sanatorium at the **Monte Palace Hotel** at the end of the 19th century.

Left: *Rainbow trout thrive in the fresh mountain spring water of Ribeiro Frio.*

CUSTARD APPLE

The custard apple (*anona*), a soft fruit which thrives in tropical and subtropical climates, was introduced to Madeira from the Caribbean. The fruit is usually heart- or almond-shaped with a yellowish brown skin and a soft and mushy pulp. Custard apples are sweet tasting and high in nutrition, containing proteins and vitamins like niacin and riboflavin. They're produced for local consumption rather than for export – you'll find them on sale at the **Mercado dos Lavradores** in Funchal as well as other island markets.

Below: *Crags, towering cliffs and deep valleys buttress Madeira's mountain centre.*

PICO DO ARIEIRO

It may come as a surprise to discover that you can drive to the summit of Madeira's third highest mountain – take the EN103 from Faial, then the EN202. The peak itself is often hidden until you emerge from the cloud drifting over the purplish moorland to bask in brilliant sunshine. From the observation point near the car park, the misty valley below Pico do Arieiro can resemble a steaming cauldron. Many first-time visitors are so impressed by the stupendous volcanic landscape that they return again and again, staying overnight in the government-run *pousada* (open during summer only – contact the tourist office in Funchal for details). To watch nature's light show as the sun rises over the peaks, bathing them in violet or vermilion hues, is an unforgettable experience. Mists descend regularly to obscure, even obliterate views, so it's advisable to make an early start if you intend walking the four-hour trip to **Pico Ruivo**, the highest point on the island at 1862m (6109ft). The path is largely paved and fenced but you'll need strong shoes, warm clothing and food – there's a café at Pico do Arieiro and a simple café below Pico Ruivo. When the visibility is good, the jagged panorama of knife-edge ridges, rift valleys and ravines almost takes your breath away. Lord of all you survey, you will find it difficult to conceive of the sun-drenched terraces and fertile coastline far below.

FAIAL

This lovely stretch of coastline is noted for its views, especially from the spectacular rock known misleadingly as **Penha de Águia** ('Eagle's Nest' – there are no eagles on Madeira). The A Chave restaurant near the church serves a good lunch of *Bacalhau na Brassa* (salted cod), *Truta no forno* (baked trout) and other Portuguese specialities, tel: 291 573 262. The new bridge over the **Ribeira Seca** opened in 1980 after its predecessor was washed away by flood water – evidence that the name 'Dry River' can be dangerously misleading. If you happen to be in this unassuming hamlet during February, look out for the **festival** celebrating the custard apple, one of many subtropical fruits that thrive on the island.

Above: *Paper flower decorations are a feature of many Madeiran festivals as seen here at Faial.*

SANTANA ★★

The hillside village of Santana is famous for its *palheiros* – distinctive, triangular-shaped cottages with steep gables and thickly thatched roofs that all but reach the ground. In days gone by the upper storey was used as an attic for storing grain or other crops. Many of the houses have suffered an ignominious fate and now serve as cowsheds; the roofs made from corrugated iron rather than thatch. Surrounded by orchards and market gardens, those that have survived make an appealing subject for a photograph, especially if you can find one with washing hanging out to dry! Santana

Above: *Pretty as a picture:* palheiros *at Santana.*

really lets its hair down for the 24 hours of the **regional folk dancing festival** early in September (check with the tourist office in Funchal for details).

Santana is the starting point for several scenic rambles. The easiest is no more than a gentle 5km (3-mile) stroll through the **Pico das Pedras National Park** to the government rest house at **Casa das Queimadas** where there's a picnic site. From here there's a signposted track through a beech and oak wood to **Pico das Pedras**; allow about 90 minutes, there and back. The alternative route along the **Levada do Caldeirão** is more demanding, though well worth the effort (the round trip takes about four hours). This 11km (7-mile) hike passes through thick virgin forest of evergreen laurel and heath trees before crossing two magnificent ravines – the **Ribeira dos Cedros** and the **Ribeira da Fonte do Louro**, where emerald mosses and lichens cling to the rock face. The highlight is the point where the **Ribeira Grande** drops 300m (984ft) into the

ARCO DO SÃO JORGE

lagoon known as the 'Green Cauldron' (**Caldeirão Verde**). Bear in mind that the path has fallen away in places, making the going slippery underfoot. You'll need a torch as there are four short tunnels to negotiate.

The **Madeira Theme Park** (open daily 10:00–19:00) is a 17-acre exhibition site devoted to the Madeiran way of life. In the pavilions you'll find eye-catching displays on sugar, wine, folklore, tourism and much else besides. Explore the grounds and you'll encounter traditional ox carts, fishing nets, a windmill and a replica of the Monte train, not to mention the maze, the boating lake and the simulator allowing you to 'travel' around the island.

ARCO DO SÃO JORGE

This tiny fishing hamlet lies at the foot of a cliff. The curving coastal ridge, which gives it its name, is not nearly as remarkable as the gorge of the Ribeira do Pôrco, which forces the EN101 to make a tortuous detour around the valley to the cliff-top village of **Boaventura** ('Good Luck'). Admire the Quinta do Arco rose garden (*see* panel, this page) and the

> ### ROSES GALORE
>
> In 2003, local horticulturalist Miguel Albuquerque began work on a pet project – to create a rose garden of unrivalled beauty in the **Quinta do Arco**. Three years later he had fulfilled his dream and visitors can now feast their eyes on more than 1200 different types of climbing and non-climbing shrubs and rose bushes, making this one of the largest collections of its kind in Portugal. The stunning scenery around Arco do São Jorge provides the perfect natural backdrop for Señor Albuquerque's handiwork and if you want to enjoy the gardens at your leisure, Quinta do Arco has accommodation available. Roseiral da Quinta do Arco, Sítio da Lagoa, Arco do São Jorge, tel: 291 570 270, open daily 11:00–18:00. For hotel reservations visit the website at www.quinta doarco.com

Left: *Ponta Delgada's church was rebuilt after a devastating fire in 1908.*

wonderful views from the *miradouro* above the village, and there's a pleasant walk to **Archada do Pereira**, starting from the church (one and a quarter hours for the round trip).

From Boaventura the main road heads west towards **Ponta Delgada** where, once again, there are outstanding views of the village – a scattering of red-roofed houses over a promontory etched with lush, green terracing. From this vantage point you'll have no problem spotting the swimming pool on the beach, within shouting distance of the waves which pound the basalt shoreline remorselessly. On the first Sunday in September the parish of **Senhor Bom Jesus** (The Good Lord Jesus) celebrates one of the most important religious festivals on the island, a favourite with Madeiran emigrants who often return at this time of year. The focus of the annual pilgrimage is a wooden crucifix which, according to tradition, was washed ashore in the 16th century. Both crucifix and church were badly damaged by fire in 1908 but the charred cross is still carried in procession on the Feast of Jesus and the Holy Sacrament. (For the rest of the year it's preserved behind glass near the west door.)

The church is also the main attraction in the village of **São Jorge** on the opposite side of the bay. The lavish interior dates from the mid-18th century and is the finest example of Baroque *talha dourada* (gilded wood-carving) outside Funchal.

Below: *The altarpiece in the church at São Jorge, a splendid example of* talha dourada.

Central Madeira at a Glance

BEST TIMES TO VISIT

August–November are best for festivals: **Chestnuts**, Curral das Freiras, early November.
Grape harvest, Câmara de Lobos, 1st half of September.
Feast of the Assumption, Monte, 14th/15th August.
Feast of Jesus and the Holy Sacrament, Ponta Delgada, 1st week of September.

GETTING THERE

Buses leave Funchal for Cabo Girão, Câmara de Lobos, Curral das Freiras (Eire), Faial, Monte, Ribeiro Frio and Santana. There is a **cable car** service linking Funchal (Campo Almirante Reis) with Monte (Largo das Babosas). Hours: winter 10:00–19:00, summer 08:30–20:30; Caminho das Barbosas 8, tel: 291 780 280, fax: 291 780 281. The **Monte toboggan** (*Carreiros do Monte*) leaves from the main square, Sítio da Igreja, tel: 291 783 919.

GETTING AROUND

The easiest way is to hire a car or taxi. Bus services, while reliable, are infrequent.

WHERE TO STAY

MID-RANGE
Pousada do Pico Arieiro, Pico do Arieiro, tel: 291 230 110, fax: 291 228 611. Guesthouse on the upper slopes of Madeira's 3rd highest mountain. A favourite with walkers.

Casa da Tia Clementina, Achada Simão Alves, Santana, tel: 291 574 144 or 226 125, fax: 291 227 526. Converted farmhouse in attractive rural setting overlooking the sea. Eight double rooms.
Quinta do Arco, Arco do São Jorge, tel: 291 570 270, website: www.quintadoarco.com Modern, secluded guesthouse in a stunning natural setting. Rooms are tastefully decorated. Also has outdoor swimming pool and rose garden.

WHERE TO EAT

LUXURY
Bacchus, Quinta do Estreito, Rua José Joaquin da Costa, Estreito da Câmara de Lobos, tel: 291 910 530. Serves international and Madeiran cuisine.
Casa da Vinha, Rua dos Lavradores 4, Estreito da Câmara de Lobos, tel: 291 945 505. Boasting wonderful coastal views, this beautifully appointed restaurant adds Gallic zest to traditional Madeiran cuisine. Try the locally produced white wine.
Quinta do Furão, Achada do Gramacho, Santana, tel: 291 570 100, website: www.quintadofurao.com Hotel-restaurant owned by the Madeira Wine Company; wine rates higher than the food.

MID-RANGE
Victor's Bar, Ribeiro Frio, tel: 291 575 898. Handy if you're about to embark on the local *levada* walk; this friendly eatery, known more formally as Ribeiro Frio restaurant, specializes in trout.

TOURS AND EXCURSIONS

Madeira Explorers, Monumental Lido, tel: 291 763 701, website: www.madeira-levada-walks.com
Heliatlantis, tel: 291 232 882, fax: 291 232 804.
Mountain Bike Hire: Joyride CC Olimpo, *see* page 59.
Diving: Clube Naval do Seixal, *see* page 77.
RR Tours, Rua Dr Pita 1A, Funchal, tel: 291 764 733, fax: 291 764 728. Jeep safaris.
Terras de Aventura e Turismo, Caminho do Amparo 25, Funchal, tel: 291 776 818, Fax: 291 771 018.
Aeroclube da Madeira, Rua do Castanheiro E2 9000-018 Funchal, tel: 291 228 311 or 964 092 580, fax: 291 221 265. Hang-gliding and paragliding.

USEFUL CONTACTS

Tourist Offices:
Câmara de Lobos, Rua Padre Eduardo Clemente Nunes Pereira, Casa de Cultura, tel: 291 943 470. Open: Monday–Friday 09:00–12:30 and 14:00–17:00, Saturday 09:30–12:00.
Santana, Sítio do Serrado, tel: 291 572 992. Open Monday–Friday 09:30–13:00, 14:30–17:30, Saturday 09:30–12:00.

5
Eastern Madeira

After Funchal, Eastern Madeira is the most densely populated part of the island. German developers began the transformation of the southern coastline between **Garajau** and **Santa Cruz** more than a decade ago. Today luxury hotels, holiday apartments, bungalows and suburban villas clutter the rocky hillsides, encouraging the traditional farming and fishing communities that eke out a living here to look to tourism as an alternative source of income. Outdoor activities are the speciality of **Caniço de Baixo**, the liveliest of these new resorts. Scuba diving is especially popular in the waters of the maritime national park at **Garajau**, but sailing, sea-fishing, tennis and golf (the **Quinta do Palheiro** course is only a 15-minute drive from **Caniço**) are all to hand. There's a lot more to the region than sport, however. The green and pleasant land of **Santo da Serra**, which incidentally boasts the island's other championship golf course, is gently wooded and excellent walking country. So too is **Portela**, where you can follow the route of the *borracheiros* (wine porters) over the mountain passes towards Funchal. One of Madeira's traditional handicrafts, wickerwork, is showcased in **Camacha**. The island's second largest town, **Machico**, is where Zarco first landed in the 15th century. The pace of life is slower here than in Funchal, but there's a beach of sorts, water-sports facilities and a few hotels – just about enough for it to qualify as a resort in its own right.

After checking out the churches and the old fort, there will still be time to explore the lush **Machico valley** and

Don't Miss

*** Quinta do Palheiro Ferreiro: magnificent subtropical gardens.
*** Ponta de São Lourenço: take a walk to the end of the island.
** Camacha: home of wickerwork.
** Machico: largest resort after Funchal.
* Caniço: swimming and scuba diving.

Opposite: *The sheltered harbour at Machico where Zarco landed in 1420.*

> ### GOLF
>
> Both Madeira's golf courses enjoy superb locations and unbeatable scenery. **Palheiro Golf**, designed by Cabell Robinson in 1993, is 6015m (6578 yards) long and par 71. **Santo da Serra Golf Club** opened in 1991 and first hosted the Madeira Open two years later. Designed by the American golf architect, Robert Trent Jones, it's 6039m (6604 yards) and par 72. Golfing equipment, including buggies, can be hired from the clubhouses, and professional tuition is available. Palheiro's facilities also include a putting green, covered training area and driving nets. A number of hotels offer discounts on course fees. For more information tel: 291 790 120 (Palheiro) or 291 550 100 (Santo da Serra); or consult the website: www.madeira-golf.com

the cliffs at **Pico do Facho**, from where there are commanding views towards the unspoilt eastern tip of the island at **Ponta de São Lourenço**.

Quinta do Palheiro Ferreiro ★★★

Within easy reach of Funchal, the magnificent **gardens** of Palheiro Ferreiro should feature on every tourist's itinerary. The *quinta* or villa (now a luxury hotel) was built for the Conde de Carvahal in 1804 and formed the centrepiece of an impressive country estate. The count's improvident descendants neglected the property but in 1885 it was saved from ruin by the wine exporter, John Blandy, who built a new mansion nearby (still the family home). The original garden was laid out in the French style: the ornamental ponds at the front of the old house and the stately avenue of plane trees and lofty camellias survive from this period. It was Blandy and his successors who introduced elements of the traditional English landscaped garden; hence the beeches, oaks and chestnuts, the herbaceous borders planted with delphiniums and day lilies, the immaculate lawns and neatly trimmed hedges. Essentially, though, Palheiro Ferreiro is a typically Madeiran subtropical garden, exemplified by the luxuriant **Jardim da Senhora** (Ladies' Garden) where the variety and sheer

QUINTA DO PALHEIRO FERREIRO

abundance of plants, shrubs and flowering trees takes the breath away: Chinese davidia, Brazilian candelabra trees, Australian jasmine, South African eaglewood, Peruvian daffodils, Madeiran geraniums and strelitzia are all represented here. Elsewhere on the estate you'll see Malaysian buddleia, giant Araucaria trees, Australian banksias and (near the Baroque chapel), the crimson-flowered waratah, emblem of New South Wales. To the rear of the old house, a path leads to the sinisterly named Ribeiro do Inferno, or Hell's River. This turns out to be nothing more menacing than a damp, rather gloomy wood planted with primitive tree ferns – watch your footing as you walk. Open Monday–Friday 09:00–16:30; tel: 291 793 044.

The remainder of the Palheiro Ferreiro estate has been re-landscaped to create one of Madeira's two championship **golf courses**, with views over Funchal Bay calculated to distract the most single-minded low handicapper (*see* panel, page 98).

Opposite: *In times gone by Pico do Facho (Torch Peak) was a lookout for pirates and would-be invaders.*

Right: *Visitors enjoying a scenic stretch of the Levada dos Tornos.*
Opposite: *Hand-woven baskets are on sale in the O Relógio shop in Camacha.*

CRICKET AND WARM BEER

The honour of founding the first **brewery** on Madeira goes to the Englishman Henry P Miles who launched what was to become a family business in 1872. (Today the beer is sold under the '**Coral**' label.) Miles was also an important promoter of the game of cricket and a founding member of the MCC (**Madeira Cricket Club**) in 1888. Cricket was first played by the sons of British businessmen, including stalwarts like the employees of the Madeira Western Telegraph Company. The first game, Bachelors v Married Men, was played at Campo de Achada, near **Camacha**, and was a great success. Cricket flourished until the end of World War I, when British influence on the island began to decline. The native Portuguese had never taken to the game, preferring soccer.

Levada dos Tornos

Madeira's longest watercourse, which is over 100km (62 miles) long, was constructed in the 1960s to supply the power station at Fajã do Nogueira. From its source, the **Ribeiro São Jorge**, the *levada* is tunneled under the peaks of the central mountain range to emerge just north of Monte. There's a scenic stretch beginning near Curral dos Romeiros and continuing for about 11km (7 miles) all the way to Camacha (allow 3½ hours); alternatively, leave the *levada* at **Palheiro Ferreiro** to visit the stunning gardens.

CAMACHA ★★

Attractively situated on a plateau surrounded by thick woodland and lush hillside terraces, Camacha is the centre of the island's **wicker-weaving industry**. The craft has a long pedigree – the builders of the first *levadas* used cane baskets, known as *barreleiros*, to carry tools, to clear debris, even to hoist themselves up the cliff face. Credit for turning the cottage industry into big business is usually given to a local mill owner, William Hinton. (Hinton's son, Harry, organized the first game of soccer in Camacha, years before the sport reached the Portuguese mainland (*see* panel, page 57). In the mid-19th century Hinton's artisans set to work imitating the cane furniture then fashionable in England and selling it to local hoteliers. Soon demand was outstripping supply as markets were found across the globe. Madeiran wickerwork is still exported to the United States, Canada, South Africa and the countries of Western Europe.

Wicker is harvested from the willow trees that thrive in the damp, humid valleys around Boaventura, where most of the plantations are located. The long, satiny shoots are soaked in water until they are supple enough to be separated from the bark. The willow is then gathered into sheaves and taken to Camacha where the workers boil the cane to make it pliable enough to fashion. The craftsmen give occasional displays in **O Relógio** (The Clock), the warehouse on the main square. Both clock and bell on the tower of this former *quinta* were presented by Dr Michael Grabham, a local naturalist, in 1896 (they originally belonged to Walton parish church in Liverpool). An obsessive collector, Grabham also donated the clock on the tower of Funchal Cathedral. Every available space in the showroom is taken up by flower baskets, picnic hampers, hats, bottle holders, furniture, trays and kitchen utensils – more than 1200 items in all. (The ingenuity of the artisans would seem to be inexhaustible.) Unfortunately the wicker dogs, deer, sheep, elephants, etc., some of which took more than six months to fashion, belong to an exhibition and are not for sale.

> **GRUPO FOLCLORICO DA CAMACHA**
>
> Camacha's famous **folk ensemble** owed its early success to the efforts of its founding director, Carlos Maria dos Santos. Dr Santos assiduously researched the traditional songs and dances of the archipelago, and his enthusiasm inspired other musicians on the island. Over the years the troupe, which celebrated its 20th anniversary in 2007, has performed at international festivals all over the world, from Holland and Estonia to Venezuela, South Africa and the United States. They spend most of their time at home, however, performing for tourists or appearing at local festivals, singing competitions, even sporting events. They've also made several recordings, available on tape or CD.

Camacha is also home to the **Grupo Folclórico da Camacha** (*see* panel, this page), an internationally acclaimed song and dance troupe.

SANTO DA SERRA

Only a 15-minute drive from Machico, Santo da Serra (**Santo António da Serra**, to give the village its full name) enjoys a spectacular setting almost 700m

> **FIRE AND BRIMSTONE**
>
> Not far from the church at **Santo da Serra** is the *quinta* once owned by the notorious **Robert Reid Kalley**. A trained doctor and part-time Protestant missionary, Kalley arrived on Madeira in 1838 and immediately began proselytizing among his poorer Roman Catholic patients. The Madeiran authorities took umbrage and in 1843 Kalley was briefly imprisoned on the orders of the governor. Unrepentant, he returned to preaching his militant brand of Presbyterianism immediately on his release. In 1846 he was forced to flee the island after a mob attacked his home and threatened his congregation. Neither chastened nor deterred, Kalley continued his missionary activities in the West Indies and was last heard of preaching to the Roman Catholics of Brazil.

(2297ft) above sea level. It was the views of the coastline around **Ponta de São Lourenço** that inspired many of Madeira's wealthier British residents to build summer retreats here in the 19th century – some of these *quintas* have since been converted to holiday lets. Farmers bring their produce to market at the weekends – the stalls line the roadside leading into the village. Near the main square is the entrance to the **Quinta do Santo da Serra**. The villa, which once belonged to the Blandy's, is closed to the public, but in the grounds there is a children's playground, a tennis court and an animal enclosure with roaming deer, goats, wild ponies and the like. Head round to the back of the estate and you'll come to a belvedere known as the **Miradouro dos Ingleses**.

The 27-hole championship **golf course** just outside the village (*see* panel, page 98) was designed by American golf architect, Robert Trent Jones, who fully exploited the natural features of the landscape and the dramatic location overlooking the Atlantic. Every spring Santo da Serra hosts the **Madeira Open**, now a major tournament and the first leg of the European PGA tour.

Right: *Santo da Serra golf course enjoys one of the most magnificent settings in Europe.*

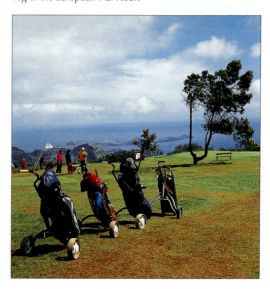

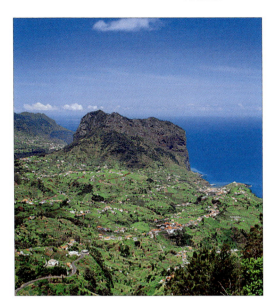

Left: *The rugged landscape from Portela to Porto da Cruz, dominated by the Penha de Águia rock.*

Portela

Driving towards Porto da Cruz, either from Funchal or Machico, it would be easy to miss Portela altogether, as it scarcely classifies as a hamlet. However, it's worth getting out of the car to stretch the legs for a few minutes, if only to admire the coastal views – **Penha de Águia** is the most obvious landmark. It can be fairly bleak when the wind gets up, but warmth and sustenance are close at hand. The homely Miradouro da Portela restaurant rustles up an excellent *espetada* (beef kebab), which goes down a treat with cider or local wine. Once rested, you may feel ready for a little walking. If so, pick up the **Levada do Portela** here, heading in the direction of the **Lamaceiros water house**. In good weather, this steady climb offers glorious views of Porto da Cruz and the neighbouring coastline. The **Levada do Serra do Faial** and the **Levada do Furado** (*see* page 88) meet at Lamaceiros. The former is one of the most popular hiking trails on Madeira, and you don't need to cover all 30km (18.6 miles) of this woodland walk to appreciate its scenic beauty.

Right: *Statue of Christ the King overlooking Ponta do Garajau.*

> ### Swimming Pools
>
> With the honourable exception of **Porto Santo**, Madeira is famous for not having sandy beaches. The rocky coastline can make swimming difficult and sometimes dangerous (especially on the north coast). The stony beaches at **Machico**, **Madalena do Mar**, **Ponta do Sol** and **Prainha** are safe for swimming. Alternatively, head for one of Madeira's eight public swimming pools:
> - Funchal (Barreirinha)
> - Funchal (Lido)
> - Funchal (Quinta Magnólia – freshwater)
> - Caniçal (Galo Mar)
> - Ponta Delgada
> - Porto da Cruz
> - Porto Moniz
> - Santa Cruz (Praia das Palmeiras)

Porto da Cruz

According to local tradition, it was the companions of naval captain Tristão Vaz Teixeira who gave this rather desolate coastal village its name by planting a cross on the shore. Porto da Cruz grew rich on the profits of the sugar trade in the 16th century. Though the plantations have long disappeared, one of the mills has survived as a distillery, turning out a potent rum-based *aguardente* (firewater). However, it's the **wine harvest** that is celebrated during the first week in September with a lively procession and general knees-up. In days gone by the porters (*borracheiros*) would tramp over the Portela pass to Funchal, toting goatskins crammed with ripened grapes. You can follow in their footsteps by picking up the trail near the village bus stop, heading towards Serrado and Cruz da Guarda. It's uphill more or less all the way to the **Miradouro da Portela** restaurant so give yourself at least two hours and wear shoes with a good grip. The rugged landscape is dominated by the brooding **Penha de Águia** rock that casts a sombre shadow over the village. For a less oppressive perspective, take the cliff-top path in the opposite direction as far as **Larano**, from where there are outstanding coastal views.

Ponta do Garajau

It was the island's first settlers who noticed flocks of terns (*garajaus*) nesting in the crevices of this formidable headland just south of Caniço. Centuries later – in 1927 to be precise – a **statue of Christ the King** (Cristo Rei) was erected on the point, recalling a similar, though much larger, monument above Rio de Janeiro. A pathway leads from the summit to the foot of the cliffs and a string of rocky coves and inlets.

The shoreline from **Lazareto Quay** in the west to **Ponta da Oliveira** in the east – 376ha (929 acres) in all – has been designated a nature reserve (**Reserva Natural Parcial do Garajau**). Conservation measures are in force here to protect the marine species that thrive in the coastal waters: groupers, moray eels, barracudas, parrot fish, trigger fish and manta rays.

Caniço ★

Caniço's strategic location between Funchal and the airport has led to it becoming one of the fastest developing tourist resorts on the island, with villas, bungalows, aparthotels and entertainment complexes encroaching from every direction. The village itself is situated a little way inland and is dominated by its **church**, a handsome building, easily distinguished by its slender campanile. Much older is the Chapel of the Mother of God at **Mãe de Deus**, founded in 1536 and with its original portal and a few other Manueline features still intact. Caniço is well served with bars and restaurants, although the majority of visitors spend more time in **Caniço de Baixo**, about 2km (1.2 miles) away at the foot of the cliff. Amenities include a mini-market as well as cafés and other eateries to the rear of the stony beach. The golf course at Palheiro is only twenty minutes' drive away and there are diving clubs at the Roca Mar Hotel and the Lido Hotel Galomar (PADI affiliated), where beginners, including children, are welcome and four- or five-day

> **Scuba Diving Centres**
>
> The most rewarding area for scuba diving is around Caniço de Baixo and Machico. Equipment can be hired from the companies listed below, but you'll need a log book, diving certificate and possibly medical certificate. Most firms also offer courses for beginners with equipment provided.
> **Manta Diving Centre**,
> Lido Hotel Galomar, Caniço de Baixo, tel/fax: 291 935 588, website: www.manta diving.com
> **Atalaia Club**, Hotel Roca Mar, Caniço de Baixo, tel: 291 934 330, fax: 291 933 011.
> **Dom Pedro Baía Club**, Machico, tel: 291 969 500, fax: 291 969 501, website: www.dompedro.com
> *See* also pages 59 and 113.

GAME FISHING

A number of firms offer deep-sea fishing trips off the coast of Madeira. Prices include the hire of equipment.
Katherine B, Traversa das Virtudes 23, tel: 291 752 685; website: www.fishmadeira.com
Margarita Lara Jade, website: www.madeira-fishing.com
Our Mary, tel/fax: 291 241 159, e-mail: madeirafishing@mail.telepac.pt

training courses are available. Scuba diving is the ideal way to enjoy the protected waters of the **Garajau natural marine park** (see panel, page 112).

Santa Cruz

The proximity of Madeira's recently expanded international airport hasn't proved a blight on this attractive village and holiday resort, now only about 15 minutes' drive from Funchal. Santa Cruz's parish church, dedicated to **São Salvador**, was built between 1479 and 1533 and is one of the largest and most appealing on the island. The **Town Hall** is almost as old as the church although only the pointed Gothic arches on the doors and windows of the façade have emerged unscathed from a succession of facelifts. Also look out for the **Law Courts** in Rua da Ponta Nova, a handsome colonial-style building dating from the 19th century, with a sweeping stone staircase, balustered verandahs and a colourful subtropical garden. Date palms and prickly dragon trees provide shade along the promenade, where you'll find seafront cafés, spotlessly clean mosaic pavements, manicured grass verges and pretty flowerbeds. The main attractions though are the **Lido** and the **Santa Cruz Aquapark** with its five toboggan rides, four fast slides, two pools, 'Lazy River' and bar.

Below: *Swimming pool terrace in the modern resort village of Caniço de Baixo. The local waters form part of the Garajau natural marine park.*

Offically opened in 2008, the **Sports Park** of Água de Pena, built under the runway of the airport, has several multi-purpose courts where it is possible to play hockey, indoor football (*futsal*), handball, basketball, volleyball, football, tennis and squash. There is also a track for sport skating and mountain biking, an area set aside for figure skating and hip-hop dancing, as well as a 12m (39ft) climbing wall; tel: 291 524 412.

Above: *The striking colonial architecture of Santa Cruz Law Court dates from the 19th century.*

Machico **

For a very brief period after the discovery of Madeira, Machico – 5km (3 miles) east of Santa Cruz – was the notional capital; it's still the most important town after Funchal, though minuscule by comparison. Machico's founder, **Tristão Vaz Teixeira**, administered the eastern side of the island from here, while Zarco governed the west. There's a statue of Teixeira in the main square, **Largo do Municipio** – local buses and taxis depart from here. Machico's impressive parish church of **Nossa Senhora da Conceição** dates from the 15th century and retains a number of Manueline features, including the portal, rose window and slender Gothic chancel arch. Dom Manuel I of Portugal himself donated the marble columns on the side door, along with an organ and various works of art. This is not quite the oldest religious foundation in the town, however; that honour goes to the **Capela dos Milagres** (Chapel of Miracles) on Largo dos Milagres, the cobbled square with a neglected air on the far side of the river. The church was renamed when a precious medieval crucifix, washed away during a flood in 1803, was recovered by American mariners out at sea. Machico's third church is dedicated to **São Roque**. Also founded in the

Free Trade Zone

The abolition of whaling in the early 1980s dealt a severe blow to the Madeiran economy. While a handful of whalemen were employed as advisors to the Society for the Protection of Marine Mammals, or as museum guides in Caniçal, the majority were forced to scrape a living from tuna fishing. To provide long-term regeneration for the area, the European Union, supported by the Portuguese and Madeiran governments, has established a Free Trade Zone, so far with mixed results.

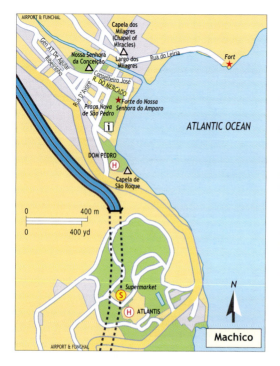

15th century, it was rebuilt in 1739 with a disproportionate Baroque doorway. It's rarely open but if you can get to see inside, there are some attractive 18th-century *azulejos*. Machico once boasted not one but three fortresses, an indication of its erstwhile importance. The triangular **Forte do Nossa Senhora do Amparo** stands in a park overlooking the sea and is open to the public. It dates from 1706 and last saw some action during the Miguelite Rebellion in 1828. Through the cobbled courtyard is Machico's **tourist office**.

The gentle shelving of the stony beach makes swimming here enjoyable, even if the water isn't quite as clean as in more secluded spots along the coast. A couple of beach cafés, and a restaurant in the former market hall, serve up tasty local fish, with spaghetti and salads. Water-sports enthusiasts can hire skis, windsurfing boards and canoes from a number of outfits along the seafront. Sailing and fishing trips can also be arranged from here. Machico is well served with bars and restaurants, mostly concentrated around the **Traversa do Mercado**, the main shopping street. Machico's red-letter days come at the end of August (when there's a torchlight procession to the Chapel of Miracles) and 8–9 October (the local carnival).

The **Largo dos Milagros** is the starting point of an enjoyable walk to the cliffs of **Pico do Facho**. As you climb the hill, there are fine views of the town and its diminutive football stadium, but nothing to compare with the panoramic vista from the top, as the peninsula tapers towards **Ponta de São Lourenço**, the most easterly point of the island. Back in the 16th century, bonfires were lit on Pico do Facho to warn the people of Machico that a pirate attack was imminent – a vital link in the chain of coastal defences.

Follow the track down to the Caniçal tunnel entrance, continue along the main road for about 15 minutes and you'll arrive at the **Levada Nova** from where you can set out to explore the lightly wooded hillsides of the Ribeira Seca valley and the terraced fields above Machico.

ROBERT MACHIN

According to legend, the first man to set foot on Madeira was Robert Machin, an **English nobleman** during the reign of Edward III (1327–77). All that is known for certain about him is that he traded with the Italian cities of Genoa and Venice and that at some point he was banished from England. The chroniclers relate how he and his mistress, Anne of Hertford, were **shipwrecked** during a storm and eventually ended up on Madeira. Machin left Anne with the crew and set off to reconnoitre the island, but during his absence the sailors abandoned the hapless woman and her page and took flight. When Anne died three days later, Robert built a chapel over the site and was eventually buried there himself. **Zarco** found the graves and named the place Machico after Machin.

Left: *Fishing is still important to the economy of Machico.*

CANIÇAL

Back in the 1950s, this sleepy fishing village, 9km (5.6 miles) northeast of Machico, was so inextricably linked with the **whaling industry** that action sequences for the film *Moby Dick* were shot off the coast here (*see* panel, page 111). In those days, Caniçal was still accessible only by boat or via a precarious cliff-top path. After the international ban on whaling in 1982, the disused station re-opened as the **Museu da Baleia** (Whaling Museum). Open Tuesday–Sunday 10:00–12:00 and 13:00–18:00; tel: 291 961 407. The exhibition tells the story of whale hunting on the island, mainly through charts and photographs. Visitors get to learn about the lives of the whalemen, the dangers they encountered on the high seas, their traditional hunting techniques, and the ritual celebrations that followed their safe return to port. The drama of the grim encounter between man and beast is thrown into stark relief by the weapons on display – harpoons, spears, ropes and grappling hooks – none of which could be used until the whale was almost under the boat. The life-size fibreglass model of a cachalot, or sperm whale, set alongside a typical open whaler, shows just how precarious the struggle could be and how prone the vessel was to capsize. The tour concludes with a 45-minute video which explains how marine biologists on the island now work hand in hand with the fishermen in conserving these beautiful creatures.

Opposite: *Whaling and the port of Caniçal were synonymous until the practice was banned in the 1980s.*

Below: *Street sellers in the pretty coastal village of Caniçal. Until 1982 when the practice was banned, most of the local fishermen earned their livelihood from whaling.*

Prainha

A side turning off the EN101-3 east of Caniçal leads to Prainha, which has the distinction of being the only **natural sand beach** on the island. Porto Santo it isn't – Prainha ('little beach' in Portuguese) is barely 100m (109yd) long, the sand is gritty and the crowds can pall on a hot summer's weekend. On the plus side, there's a café-bar, showers and good swimming in and around the inlet.

Perched on the crest of a hill overlooking the beach is the **Capela de Nossa Senhora de Piedade** that was built at the expense of local fishermen in 1921. Once a year, on the third Sunday of September, a statue of the Virgin is carried in procession from the parish church in Caniçal to the shore, from where it is escorted by a flotilla of brightly decorated boats to the chapel at Prainha.

Ponta de São Lourenço ★★★

The most relaxing way to see Madeira's most easterly point is to take the **boat trip** from Funchal to Ponta do Furado, viewing **Garajau**, **Caniço de Baixo**, **Machico** and **Caniçal** en route. Alternatively, follow the EN101-3 to the car park just before Baía de Abra and walk. Bear in mind that this is quite a demanding hike and you'll need to be

Moby Dick

Released in 1956, the film *Moby Dick* was directed by John Huston and starred Gregory Peck and Orson Welles. Only the opening sequences were shot on Madeira owing to rough weather – the crew decamped to Youghal, off the coast of Ireland, for the other whaling scenes. Ray Bradbury's screenplay was based on Herman Melville's classic tale of Captain Ahab's obsession with taking revenge on the whale that had taken off his leg on an earlier expedition. Craving authenticity Huston and Peck (though not Welles it seems), befriended the whalers of **Caniçal** who, after some persuasion, took them on a whaling expedition. Despite seasickness, both men relished the experience and returned to Reid's Hotel impressed with the crew's courage and strength.

Above: *Ponta de São Lourenço, the easternmost point on the island.*

> ### DIVING SITES
>
> Madeira's coastal waters support a rich marine life. Visibility is excellent – up to 50m (164ft) at Ponta de São Lourenço – which accounts for the growing number of scuba-diving schools. Most are based around **Caniço de Baixo**, popular due to its proximity to Machico Bay and the **Garajau** natural marine park. Here you may encounter monkfish, barracudas, octopus, sea spiders, eels, manta rays, the great locust lobster and other species that thrive in Atlantic waters. The clubs offer courses with equipment provided. Wreck and night dives are also organized.

properly equipped. Today the peninsula is almost barren, the vermilion-tinged rock reminiscent of the Martian landscape in places, but it was not always so. In the days of the first settlers the area was heavily forested but the soil never recovered once the trees were uprooted to provide more land for pasture. Each spring, however, Ponta de São Lourenço comes abruptly to life as a rash of flowers breaks out miraculously among the scrub. From the observation point below the car park you'll be able to make out land's end and the lighthouse beyond, left high and dry on its own jagged islet (**Ilhéu do Farol**). There are equally compelling views as the footpath follows the curve of the bay, notably at 'Sea Horses', a triangular rock formation off the north coast, and at 'Seagull's Peak' (at Ponta das Gaivotas), about 300m (984ft) above the pounding Atlantic Ocean. Take your binoculars to appreciate the bird life of the peninsula: terns, Cory's shearwaters, little egrets, buzzards, whimbrels, kestrels and rock doves are all regular visitors. The going gets tougher, and the terrain more vertiginous, beyond the house at **Casa Sardinhas** – a favourite picnic spot, where you may want to call it a day.

Eastern Madeira at a Glance

BEST TIMES TO VISIT

July–October are best for festivals: **Feast of the onion**, Caniço, mid-August.
Gastronomy week, Machico, end July, beginning August.
Carnival (Feast of the Holy Sacrament), Machico, last weekend in August.
Grape harvest, Porto da Cruz, 1st week of September.
Apple harvest, Santo da Serra, 1st week of September. **Feast of Our Lord of Miracles**, Machico, 9 October.

GETTING THERE

Buses leave Funchal for Camacha, Caniçal, Caniço, Garajau, Machico, Porto da Cruz, Santa Cruz, Santo da Serra, Quinta do Palheiro Ferreiro. To reach Prainha and São Lourenço take the bus to Caniçal, then a taxi.

GETTING AROUND

Since bus services are infrequent either **hire a car** or **taxi**.

WHERE TO STAY

LUXURY
Quinta Splendida, Estrada da Ponte Oliveira 11, Caniço, tel: 291 930 400, fax: 291 930 401, website: www.quintasplendida.com This modern hotel in the village occupies the grounds of a historic *quinta*.
Roca Mar, Caminho Cais da Oliveira, Caniço de Baixa, tel: 291 934 334, fax: 291 934 044. Resort hotel with diving, pools, evening entertainment and shuttle bus to Funchal.

MID-RANGE
Estalagem do Santo, Casais Próximos 9200, Santo António da Serra, tel: 291 550 550, fax: 291 550 505. Modern, handy for Santo da Serra golf course.
Dom Pedro Garajau, Estrada do Garajau, Caniço, tel: 291 930 800, fax: 291 930 801, website: www.dompedro.com Reliable, convenient for local resorts.
Pensão Amparo, Rua da Amargura, Machico, tel: 291 968 120, fax: 291 966 050. Small, friendly, near beach.

WHERE TO EAT

LUXURY
Casa Velha do Palheiro, Estalagem Casa Velha do Palheiro, Palheiro Golf, São Gonçalo, tel: 291 790 350, website: www.casa-velha.com French chef gives classic Portuguese dishes a makeover.
La Perla, Quinta Splendida, Estrada da Ponte Oliveira 11, Caniço, tel: 291 930 401. Mediterranean cuisine with organically grown ingredients.

MID-RANGE
Miradouro da Portela, Portela 9225, Porto da Cruz, tel: 291 966 169. Good-value home cooking, near the well-known viewing point.
Atlantis, Ondamar Hotel, Ponta da Oliveira, Aptdo 12, Caniço, tel: 291 930 930. Popular hotel restaurant featuring fresh tuna and swordfish.
Quinta do Lorde, Sítio da Piedade, Aptdo 530, tel: 291 960 200, website: www.quintadolorde.com Restaurant on the marina serving tasty Portuguese and international dishes.

BUDGET
Hortensia Gardens, Caminho dos Pretos 89, São João Latrão, tel: 291 792 179. Tearooms on the Levada dos Tornos.

TOURS AND EXCURSIONS

Heliatlantis, see page 59. There is a **boat excursion** from Funchal marina to Ponta de São Lourenço, with a stopover at Caniçal for lunch.
Jet Ski / Water Ski: Nautileste, Praça da Praia, Machico, tel/fax: 291 965 248.
Diving: Manta Diving Centre, Lido Hotel Galomar, Caniço de Baixo, tel/fax: 291 935 588; Atalaia Club, Hotel Roca Mar, Caniço de Baixo, tel: 291 934 330. **Motorcycle and bike rental:** Magos Bike, Caniço de Baixo, tel: 291 934 818, fax: 291 934 819, website: www.magoscar.com

USEFUL CONTACTS

Tourist Offices: Madeira International Airport, tel: 291 524 933. Open daily 09:00–24:00; **Caniço de Baixo**, tel: 291 932 919. Open Monday–Friday 09:30–13:00, 14:30–17:30, Saturday 09:30–12:00;
Machico, Forte Nossa Senhora do Amparo, tel: 291 962 289. Open Monday–Friday 09:00–12:30, 14:00–17:00, Saturday 09:30–12:00.
Quinta do Lorde Marina, (4km from Caniçal). Yachting and excursions; tel: 291 960 200.

6
Porto Santo

Just 11km (6.8 miles) long and 7km (4.3 miles) wide, the island of Porto Santo lies some 40km (25 miles) northeast of Madeira, but the landscape couldn't be more different. Madeira's satellite is more like a desert island – parched, arid and for the most part flat, hence the soubriquet 'tawny isle'. The 5000 inhabitants have the place to themselves for most of the year, but in August the picture changes as Madeirans and mainland Portuguese arrive in numbers for the summer vacation. The attraction is the 9km (5.6 miles) of **pure golden sand** extending along the southern coastline. The climate too is ideal, with very little rainfall, generous amounts of sunshine, and warm sea temperatures. Hiring a bike could be the best way to see the island, but there are also boat trips, taxi tours and a couple of hiking trails. You can climb at least two of the peaks (**Pico do Facho** and **Pico do Castelo**), while **Morenos**, the greenest spot, and **Fonte da Areia**, the island's mini-spa, are great for picnics. Bird-watchers too have a field day here – hoopoes, black-headed gulls, snipe, plovers, sandpipers, sanderlings, wagtails, pipits and rock sparrows have all been sighted.

Christopher Columbus is said to have lived on Porto Santo for a time – his house is the only real tourist site in the island capital of **Cidade Vila Baleira**.

CIDADE VILA BALEIRA ★★★

There's little natural shade on the **beach** so bring plenty of sunblock and a head covering. Swimming in the warm, translucent waters is an unadulterated pleasure, the soft

DON'T MISS

★★★ **The beach:** 9km (5.6 miles) of golden sand.
★★ **Boat trip** along the coast.
★★ **Pico do Castelo:** A difficult climb but excellent views.
★★ **Calheta:** remarkable sunsets.
★★ **Fonte da Areia:** health-giving springs.
★★ **Morenos:** greenest spot on the 'tawny isle'.

Opposite: *The beach at Porto Santo. Soft sand underfoot makes a welcome change from the stony shelving of Madeiran beaches.*

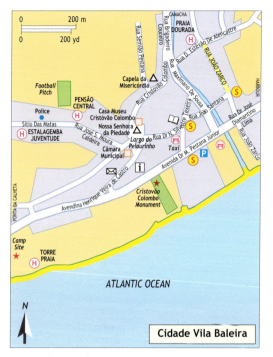

Cidade Vila Baleira

sand underfoot making a welcome change after the stony shelving of Madeiran beaches. Amenities include several cafés, showers, toilets and palm umbrellas. For a more active holiday, enquire at the tourist office for details of the **diving school** (beginners are welcome), the three-hour **boat excursion** around the island (dolphin sightings are promised), and the deep-sea **fishing trips** in search of blue marlin. Windsurfing, paragliding, volleyball and donkey rides are also available, depending on the weather and the season, while the larger hotels such as the Hotel Vila Baleira and the Porto Santo offer tennis courts, mini-golf and gymnasiums. At Hotel Vila Baleira there is even a thalassotherapy centre where marine products are used for therapeutic treatments.

At the heart of the tiny port of Vila Baleira is the sand-blown square, **Largo do Pelourinho**, where the unassuming whitewashed houses, dressed with pink oleander, are shaded by palms and dragon trees. The entrepreneurial-minded early settlers soon discovered that the sap from the latter, known as *sangue de drago* (dragon's blood), could be exploited commercially as a fabric dye. The Morgada chapel in the parish church of **Nossa Senhora da Piedade** dates from the time of the discoverers, anticipating Vila Baleira's **town hall** by about 100 years.

Just behind the square, on Rua Cristovão Colombo, is the **Christopher Columbus House Museum**. While there's no documentary proof that the great explorer lived here, it

CULINARY FAVOURITES

Many restaurants in **Vila Baleira** (Porto Santo) specialize in fish dishes. Stewed or roasted parrot fish is one delicacy, while the stew *fragateria*, sometimes translated as 'kettle of fish', is also worth trying. Surprisingly, given the arid landscape, Porto Santo also produces Verdelho and Malvasia wines, harvested as early as August owing to the warmth of the sun and the sandy soil. Production has been increasing in recent years.

is certain that he visited Porto Santo in or around 1478 and that he married the daughter of Bartolomeu Perestrelo, Filipa Moniz. Anyone looking for evidence of the couple's day-to-day life here, however, will be disappointed – the small exhibition consists mainly of reproductions – charts, engravings and unauthenticated portraits. It is open July, August, September, Tuesday–Saturday 10:00–12:30, 14:00–19:00, Sunday 10:00–13:00; tel: 291 983 405.

Ponta da Calheta ★★

Beyond the *miradouro* at Ponta da Calheta, Porto Santo's seemingly infinite expanse of glistening sand finally comes to an end, giving way to a more ragged coastline of bays, coves and inlets more typical of Madeira. Set out from Vila Baleira late in the afternoon and revel in the spectacular sunsets and views of **Ilhéu de Baixo**, one of Porto Santo's island satellites. The terrace of the Pôr do Sol restaurant is a perfect place to relax over a meal of grilled fish, washed down by a bottle of local Verdelho.

Fonte da Areia ★★

To visit the springs at Fonte da Areia take the bus to Camacha and walk. The **therapeutic** properties of the water that seeps from Porto Santo's mineral-rich sandstone

> **ENDANGERED SPECIES**
>
> Also known as the 'sea wolf' (*Lobo Marinho*), the monk seal is currently one of the five most endangered species on the planet. Apart from the **Desertas**, where there are around 20 pairs at present, the main breeding grounds are the Aegean and the north coast of Morocco. Closed-circuit television cameras have been installed on the Desertas to monitor the seals' progress. Persistent culling by fishermen led them to take refuge in caves along the coast but recently (and highly unusually) there have been seals on the beach itself, their natural habitat. There are also encouraging signs that reproduction is beginning to take off again, after several disappointing years.

Below: *The beach on Porto Santo is said to have health-giving properties.*

Prophets

The people of **Porto Santo** are often referred to as *profétas* (prophets). The name dates back to the 16th century when a crazed settler, Fernão Nunes, became convinced that he and his niece, Filipa, had been instructed by God to bring the inhabitants to repentance. Apparently, he was assisted in his task by the uncanny knack of being able to itemize the sins of any person he encountered – though the locals were probably more impressed by his ability to heal the sick (Filipa was apparently cured of paralysis). It wasn't long before the hullabaloo reached the ears of the Madeiran authorities, who promptly despatched a magistrate to make arrests. Thereafter the movement subsided as the leaders, including several priests, were taken to Portugal for punishment.

Golfing Latest

Madeira's newest golf course, located at the foot of Pico Ana Ferreira, was officially opened in October 2004. Designed by Severiano Ballesteros, it will be the largest in the archipelago when finished. Golf enthusiasts are queuing to tee off on the two 72-par, 9-hole circuits and the illuminated, nine par-3 pitch and putt holes. Facilities include a driving range, putting and chipping greens, pro shop and Jacuzzi. **Porto Santo Golfe**, Sitio das Marinhas, Porto Santo, tel: 291 983 778, fax: 291 983 777, website: www.portugalgolf.pt

---

have long been known, and a long-sceptical medical profession now recognizes the benefits. Rheumatism, varicose veins, kidney ailments, eczema, even bone diseases are thought to respond to its curative properties. In the 19th century, when spa towns were the rage in Europe, drinking fountains were installed at Fonte da Areia and other strategic points across the island – you may already have tasted the mineral water, as it's widely available in Madeira's restaurants. Soak up the coastal views from the snack bar alongside the fountain, before taking a closer look at the cliffs – Fonte da Areia's other point of interest. Wind and rain erosion have created natural sculptures and weird and wonderful patterns on the soft, flaky sandstone. A path descends from the cliff top to a small pebble beach with rock pools.

A Tour of the Island

Vila Baleira is often referred to as Porto Santo, its original name. According to the Portuguese chronicle, *Saudades da Terra*, when the sea captains Zarco and Teixeira were washed up on the island after being blown off course during a storm, they named their place of refuge Porto Santo, meaning 'holy' or 'blessed' port.

Hire a car or a taxi and in half a day you'll be able to see most of what the island has to offer; alternatively, hire a bike or a motorcycle (don't forget your sunglasses, sunblock and water bottle).

Leave Vila Baleira on Rua Bispo de Alencastre and follow the signs to **Serra de Fora**. The road skirts around the Vale do Touro, passing a turnoff to the Chapel of Nossa Senhora da Graça (founded 1533), on the way to the *miradouro* at **Portela** about 2km (1.2 miles) further. The landmark here is a spindle-and-sail **windmill**, one of a number dotted about the island, used originally for grinding corn. The observation point affords views of the celebrated beach to the west, and of the cone-shaped Pico de Baixo and Ilhéu de Cima (complete with lighthouse) to the east.

Beyond Serra de Fora is the broad valley of the **Serra de Dentro**. The efforts of local farmers to eke out a living

A TOUR OF THE ISLAND

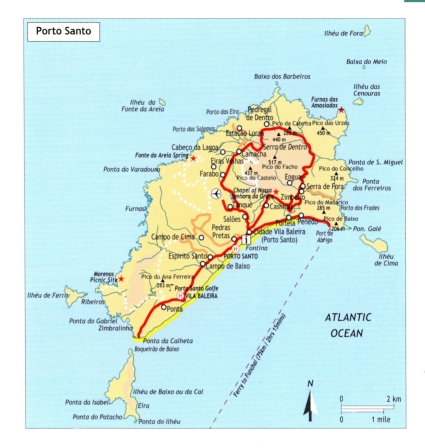

from crops grown on the hillsides have been frustrated by the perennial shortage of water. Traditionally the limestone houses here were covered with the dark grey clay known as *salão*. During the summer, the clay dries and cracks appear, allowing the air to circulate, while in winter *salão* absorbs the rain like a sponge.

The Estrela do Norte (Northern Star) restaurant is the only reason to linger in the hamlet of **Camacha**. From here you could take the side road to **Fonte da Areia** (*see* page 117). Otherwise leave Camacha in the direction of **Pico do Castelo**, named for its now ruined fort which was built

Above: *Windmills on Porto Santo were once a familiar part of the landscape but are now a rarity.*

> **PORTO SANTO – WHAT TO BUY**
>
> **Palm weaving** (*entrançados de palmitos*), a craft exclusive to the island, uses the leaves of the *Phoenix canariensis*. It is a dying art, sustained by a few women from a single village (Serra de Fora). Hats are the most common item but you'll also see wallets, belts, bottle covers, etc., sold in the shops of **Vila Baleira** or from roadside stalls. Other craft items include cane baskets, nativity figures made from *salão* (a clay also used for insulating houses), and wooden models of Porto Santo's windmills.

in the 16th century to defend the island against pirate attack – with little success, judging by the historical records. Pico do Castelo is a fairly arduous climb in hot weather, so don't set out without a water bottle. From here you could hike to the next hilltop, Pico do Facho, for even better views. The name, Torch Peak, is a reminder of the days when bonfires warned settlers that the corsairs were approaching. (One refuge for the fleeing population was **Furnas das Amasiadas**, a cave on the northeastern coast where the pits for storing food can still be seen.)

From Pico do Castelo, either return to Vila Baleira and call it a day, or take the beach road to the west of the town. Looking right, after a couple of minutes you'll notice the tawny-coloured mound, Pico de Ana Ferreira, named after an illegitimate daughter of Dom João II of Portugal. The road runs out at **Ponta da Calheta** (*see* page 117). Two other beauty spots could be explored from here: the secluded pebble beach at **Zimbralinho**, and **Morenos**, one of the greenest spots on the island and good for picnicking.

ILHAS DESERTAS

The '**Desert Islands**' (Deserta Grande, Ihéu Chão and Búgio) lie approximately 30km (19 miles) off the coast of Madeira, from where they are often visible. There was a time, centuries ago, when Deserta Grande was inhabited, though the barren terrain and arduous conditions soon drove the settlers away, leaving the mountain goats, rabbits and the giant, highly venomous black spider, *Lycosa ingens*, to fend for themselves. Since 1990, when the islands were claimed as a nature reserve, no one has been allowed to land without a government permit. The Desertas are not completely out of bounds, however – when sea conditions are favourable it's possible to join one of the boat excursions exploring the **coastal waters**. While you're unlikely to spot the monk seals, an endangered species, you will see the colonies of sea birds, including Atlantic shearwaters and petrels – the soft-plumed petrel being indigenous to these islands. For the best sightings, come between April and mid-November.

Porto Santo at a Glance

Best Times to Visit

Porto Santo enjoys pretty much year-round **sunshine** and the temperature rarely falls below 20°C (68°F). The crowds arrive in July and disperse at the beginning of September. At other times of the year, you'll have the island more or less to yourself.

Getting There

The *Lobo Marinho* (Sea Wolf) **ferry** from Funchal to Porto Santo (daily except Tuesdays October–June) takes about 2½ hours. Pre-booking is essential in July and August. It's also possible to reach Porto Santo by **catamaran** (1½ hours). From the port, **taxis** deliver guests to hotels, otherwise it's a short walk to the near (eastern) end of the beach. There are several expensive **flights** daily from Funchal airport (takes 15 minutes). Buy tickets from any travel agent or branches of TAP, the Portuguese national airline. Pre-booking is essential in high season.

Getting Around

The easiest way is to **hire a car**, a **taxi** or even a **bike**.

Where to Stay

Luxury
Hotel Vila Baleira, Sítio do Cabeço da Ponta Apt do 243 9400-090, Porto Santo, tel: 291 980 800, fax: 291 980 801, website: www.vilabaleira.com New high-rise with thalassotherapy centre, out- and indoor pools and beach club.
Porto Santo Hotel, Campo de Baixo 9400-015, tel: 291 980 140, fax: 291 980 149. Features a bar, restaurant, pool, tennis court, mini-golf and windsurfing.
Luamar, Cabeço da Ponta 9400-030, 4km (2.5 miles) from Vila Baleira, tel: 291 984 121, fax: 291 983 100. Over 100 self-catering apartments with satellite TV, snack bar, tennis court, sauna and pool.

Where to Eat

Mid-range
Mar e Sol, Campo de Baixo, tel: 291 982 269. Seafood restaurant near the Porto Santo Hotel.
Pôr do Sol, Ponta da Calheta, tel: 291 984 380. Terrace restaurant serving fish dishes.
La Roca, Porto do Abrigo, tel: 291 982 353. Classy and romantic ranch-style restaurant overlooking the marina.

Entertainment

While many visitors are happy with an after-dinner stroll along the beach, there's no shortage of night-time entertainment in Vila Baleira. There is a cluster of lively bars and clubs in the harbour area known as Peneda do Sono. **Apollo 14** pub on the main square (open till 02:00) is quieter. Salsa enthusiasts gather at **La Siesta** on the beach. The restaurant and bar of the **La Roca Yacht Club** has a verandah overlooking the sea. **Quinta do Serrado** offers live music every evening while the **Porto Santo Hotel** is a venue for jazz. There are currently two discos on the island: **Challenger**, Rua D. Esteva de Alencastre, and **Big Boy**, Rua João Santana.
Clube Naval do Porto Santo, 9400 Porto Santo, tel/fax: 291 982 085. Boat and canoe trips.
Sports: Porto Santo offers every conceivable sport, from surfing and hang-gliding to tennis and golf. Contact the tourist office for more details.

Useful Contacts

Car Rental: Rodavante, Aeroporto do Porto Santo, tel: 291 982 925.
Tourist Office: Avenida Henrique Veira e Castro 5, Vila Baleira, tel: 291 982 361. Open Monday–Friday 09:00–17:30, Saturday 10:00–12:30.
Post Office, Avenida Henrique Veira de Castro, tel: 291 980 011.
Police, tel: 291 982 423.
Porto Santo Airport, tel: 291 980 120, fax: 291 980 121, website: www.anam.pt
TAP Air Portugal, Avenida das Comunidades Madeirenses 8–10, Funchal Airport, tel: 291 520 835, website: www.tap-airportugal.com
Porto Santo Line, Rua da Praia 4, Funchal, tel: 291 210 300, fax: 291 226 434, website: www.portosantoline.pt

Travel Tips

Tourist Information
Funchal Tourist Office, Avenida Arriaga 18, tel: 291 211 900, fax: 291 232 151. See At a Glance pages for offices in other areas; e-mail info@madeiratourism.org or see www.madeiratourism.org
Portugal, Lisboa Welcome Centre, Praça do Comércio, Lisbon, tel: 21 031 2815.
Canada, 60 Bloor Street West, Suite 1005, Toronto, Ontario, M4W 3B8, tel: 416 921 7376, fax: 416 921 1353. 2075 University, Suite 1206, Montreal, Quebec H3A 2L1, tel: 514 282 1264, fax: 514 499 1450.
South Africa, 4th Floor, Sunnyside Ridge, Sunnyside Drive, Parktown, PO Box 2473, Houghton 2041, Johannesburg, tel: 2711 484 3487, fax: 2711 484 5416.
UK, 11 Belgrave Square, London SW1X 8PP, tel: 0845 355 1212, fax: 020 7201 6633, website: www.visitportugal.com
USA, Portuguese National Tourist Office, 590 Fifth Avenue, 4th Floor, New York, NY 10036–4785, tel: 212 354 4403, fax: 212 764 6137.

Entry Requirements
Every visitor must be in possession of a valid passport. Citizens of European Union countries, Canada, the United States of America or Japan do not require a visa; other nationalities should contact their Portuguese consulate for all stays of up to 90 days.

Customs
Portugal, as a member of the European Union, is subject to its customs regulations. Limits are imposed on goods obtained duty free within the EU and on goods bought outside the EU. Other items bought within the EU are governed by 'guidance levels' which recommend amounts considered to be for personal use. Narcotics, firearms and other weapons, obscene material and unlicensed animals are all prohibited.

Health Requirements
No special immunizations are required, or necessary. There is no free health service on Madeira, so it is recommended that you take out medical insurance to cover emergencies. Make sure you keep receipts if you intend to make a claim. EU citizens should take their EHIC card that enables them to claim a refund on basic healthcare.

Air Travel
Madeira International airport handles flights from most European destinations, either direct or via Lisbon. The flight time is about 3 hours 40 minutes from London. As flying is the only way to enter Madeira, most flights are fully booked, especially during the summer. The airport is 18km (10.5 miles) from the capital, Funchal – an aerobus runs to the city approximately every two hours. Madeira airport information, tel: 291 524 941/ 520 700.

What to Take
Take clothing that covers all eventualities. In the summer, dress for hot weather with a jacket or jumper for evenings. Always take something waterproof – it may rain at any time. If you are planning to walk along a *levada* or in the mountains you will need stout

shoes or walking boots. Don't forget a sun hat, sun cream, water bottle and a camera.

Money Matters

Euro bank notes and coins were introduced into Portugal on 1 January 2002 to replace the Portuguese currency, the escudo. Exchange rates for visitors from outside the euro zone are clearly displayed in banks, currency exchange offices and hotels.

Coins are issued in denominations of 1, 2, 5, 10, 20 and 50 euro cents and 1 and 2 euros. Notes are issued in denominations of 5, 10, 20, 50, 100, 200 and 500 euros.

All major credit cards and traveller's cheques are widely accepted in shops, restaurants and hotels. Banks and ATM cashpoints can be found in Funchal and the larger towns across the island (look for the MB sign). Tipping is not generally expected on Madeira and most hotels and restaurant bills include service as well as IVA (VAT). A small tip (10%) for good service can be left at your discretion.

Accommodation

Most hotels are concentrated in Funchal (especially the Hotel Zone – the cliff-top area, west of the town). However, there is a fair sprinkling of accommodation throughout the island. Rooms cover all price ranges – generally, the further you are from the centre of town, the less you have to pay. You may be charged extra for a sea view. There are aparthotels and other types of self-catering accommodation along the Estrada Monumental in Funchal and elsewhere on the island, especially in the Caniço area. A small rural hotel is often called a *residencial* or **estalagem**. They are often family-run and include converted *quintas*. **Pousadas** are inns owned by the Portuguese government. There are two on Madeira, both enjoying fabulous locations: one on the slopes of the Pico do Arieiro, the other in the wooded Serra da Agua Valley. Both are extremely popular and must be booked well in advance. There are two official **camp sites** on the island, in Porto Moniz and Montado do Pereiro. It is also possible to camp in the nature reserve at Montado do Pereiro, but you need a permit from the forest wardens. There is another camp site on Porto Santo. Contact Madeira Camping Service, tel: 291 776 726/7, fax: 291 762 003, website: www.madeira-camping.com

Eating Out

Most restaurants in Funchal are open 11:00–23:00, although some close in the late afternoon and reopen for dinner at 19:00. Many small bars stay open until 04:00. It's possible to eat well without burning a hole in your pocket. The more expensive restaurants tend to serve international cuisine, but you will find some excellent regional cooking in the mid-range establishments while every-

> **PUBLIC HOLIDAYS AND FESTIVALS**
>
> There are many festivals on Madeira; some are national holidays, others local celebrations of saints' days. Bands, folklore groups, decorated boats and street banners are some of the things to look out for.
> **1 January** • New Year
> **February** • Carnival (celebrated in towns throughout the island)
> **March/April** • Shrove Tuesday, Ash Wednesday, Good Friday, Easter Monday
> **April** • Flower Festival, Funchal
> **25 April** • Day of the Revolution
> **1 May** • Labour Day
> **June** • Corpus Christi
> **10 June** • National Day
> **1 July** • Madeira Day
> **15 August** • Feast of the Assumption (widely celebrated, especially in Monte)
> **21 August** • Funchal Day
> **September** • Apple Festival (Ponta do Pargo and Camacha)
> **September** • Wine Festival (Estreito da Câmara de Lobos, Funchal and Porto da Cruz)
> **5 October** • Republic Day
> **1 November** • All Saints' Day, Chestnut Festival (in Curral das Freiras)
> **1 December** • Restoration of Independence Day
> **8 December** • Immaculate Conception
> **25 December** • Christmas
> **31 December** • Firework display in Funchal harbour

where there are bars and cafés serving traditional Madeiran dishes as well as a variety of snacks.

Transport

Air: There are internal flights from Funchal to Porto Santo (five a day). Flight time is 15 minutes. Book well in advance in high season through a travel agent or TAP Air Portugal, Avenida das Comunidades Madeiranses 8–10, tel: 291 239 211, website: www.tap-airportugal.pt

Road: Visitors cannot easily bring their own cars to Madeira; consequently there are numerous rental firms offering competitive rates. You can book a car in advance, on arrival at the airport, or through your hotel. The best deals are via the Internet: see www.RentalCarGroup.com or www.Carhire.co.uk or try Avis, tel: 291 524 392.

Age restrictions vary according to the car hire firm. Negotiating the narrow mountain roads can be taxing, especially when approaching the more popular sights where tour coaches are an additional hazard on hairpin bends.

Most companies operate their own breakdown services and will explain the procedures in the event of a breakdown. It is essential to take out damage waiver insurance if this is not included in the deal.

Drive on the right-hand side of the road and give way to vehicles approaching from the right. The speed limit on motorways is 120kph (75mph), on major roads 90kph (55mph) and in town 50kph (31mph). It is mandatory for drivers and passengers to wear seat belts. Children under 12 must travel in the rear. The blood to alcohol limit is 0.05%; more than 0.12% will result in imprisonment. Petrol is available in two grades; lead-free and LPG. Most villages have a garage or at least a petrol pump (open 08:00–20:00), but it's a good idea to fill up before you leave Funchal. The GALP petrol station on Avenida do Infante is open 24 hours.

Taxis: Taxis are bright yellow with a distinctive blue stripe down the side. There are ranks in every town and taxis may also be flagged down at the roadside. Short trips are metered. Rates for certain out-of-town journeys (e.g. to the airport) are fixed and may include waiting times. There are surcharges for extra luggage and for travelling between 22:00 and 07:00, or on Sundays and public holidays. Hourly or half-day rates can be negotiated for longer journeys. In Funchal taxi ranks can be found on Avenida do Mar, Avenida Arriaga, Largo do Municipio and elsewhere.

Buses: There are reliable bus connections between Funchal and all of the main towns and villages. Buses are modern and comfortable and have a good safety record. There are a number of private operators. Municipal buses in Funchal are orange. The main bus stops, also ticket kiosks, are on Avenida do Mar – cancel your ticket in the machine as you board the bus. Seven-day 'go as you please' passes are valid on all routes and are available to visitors on presentation of a passport. For timetable info visit www.busstation.net

Boats: The Porto Santo Line ferry departs from Funchal harbour daily around 08:00. The journey takes about 2 hours 30 minutes. Tickets can be bought in advance from travel agents or from the jetty just before sailing. For information, contact Porto Santo Line, Rua da Praia 6, Funchal, tel: 291 210 300, fax: 291 226 434. Don't leave buying your ticket till the last minute during high season. Half- or full-day sightseeing cruises along the coast leave from the yachting marina. Sea fishing trips, charter and evening cruises (with dinner) are also available.

Conversion Chart

From	To	Multiply By
Millimetres	Inches	0.0394
Metres	Yards	1.0936
Metres	Feet	3.281
Kilometres	Miles	0.6214
Square kilometres	Square miles	0.386
Hectares	Acres	2.471
Litres	Pints	1.760
Kilograms	Pounds	2.205
Tonnes	Tons	0.984

To convert Celsius to Fahrenheit: $x \times 9 \div 5 + 32$

Useful Phrases

Hello • *Olá*
Goodbye • *Adeus*
Good morning • *Bom dia*
Good afternoon • *Boa tarde*
Good evening / night • *Boa noite*
Please • *Se faz favor*
Thank you • *Obrigado / a*
Yes • *Si*
No • *Não*
How much is it? • *Quanto custa isto?*
Where is the…? • *Onde fica…?*
I'm lost • *Perdi-me*

I don't understand • *No compréndo*
Can you help me? • *Ajude-me, por favor*
What time is it please? • *Que horas são, por favor?*
Can I have… • *Posso eu ter...*
hotel • *hotel / estalagem*
bill • *conta*
bank • *um banco*
Can you change…? • *Pode trocar..?*
post office • *correio*
airport • *aeroporto*
bus stop • *paragem*

A ticket to…. • *Um bilhete para…*
Where's the bus for…? • *Onde está o auto carro para…?*

1 • *um (uma)*
2 • *dois (duas)*
3 • *três*
4 • *quatro*
5 • *cinco*
6 • *seis*
7 • *sete*
8 • *oito*
9 • *nove*
10 • *dez*
11 • *onze*
12 • *doze*

13 • *treze*
14 • *catorze*
15 • *quinze*
16 • *dezasseis*
17 • *dezassete*
18 • *dezoito*
19 • *dezanove*
20 • *vinte*
21 • *vinte e um*
30 • *trinta*
40 • *quarenta*
50 • *cinquenta*
60 • *sessenta*
70 • *setenta*
80 • *oitenta*
90 • *noventa*
100 • *cem/cento*
1000 • *mil*

Business Hours
Shops: Normal opening hours are Monday–Friday 09:00–13:00 and 15:00–19:00, Saturday 09:00–13:00. Larger outlets and shops in tourist areas tend to stay open through lunch and until 22:00. Shopping centres are open daily (including Sunday) 10:00–22:00. Pharmacies (*farmacia*) – look for the green cross symbol – have a 24-hour opening rota on the shop door.
Museums: Opening times vary, but 10:00–12:30 and 14:30–18:00 are fairly standard. Check whether there is a closing day before you set out.
Business hours: Monday–Friday 09:00–17:00.
Banks: Open Monday–Friday 08:30–15:00. Some open Saturday 09:00–12:30.
Main **post offices**: open Monday–Friday 08:30–20:00 and Saturday 09:00–12:30, smaller branches only open Monday–Friday 09:00–18:00. Most shops close on Sundays and public holidays. Generally, restaurants stay open, except on Christmas Day.

Time Difference
Madeira operates GMT (Greenwich Mean Time) in the summer and, along with the rest of the EU, puts the clock back one hour on the last Sunday of October and forward one hour on the last Sunday in March.

Communications
There are telephone kiosks on the main streets of Funchal and Machico. Many bars and restaurants have pay phones. Some only take phonecards that can be purchased from newsagents or on the premises, others take coins and a few even credit cards. International calls from the island are expensive, especially if made from a hotel. The international code for Madeira (Portugal) is 351 and the area code 291. There are special rates for long-distance calls between midnight and 08:00. There are post offices (*correios*) in all the main towns on Madeira and Porto Santo. The main post offices in Funchal are on Avenida do Zarco, tel: 291 202 830, and Rua Dr Brito Câmara. They handle telegrams, telexes, faxes and telephone calls as well as mail. The main office in Porto Santo is in Vila Baleira (Avenida Vieira Castro). Postage stamps are also on sale at most newsagents.

Most European **mobile phones** work on Madeira and coverage is generally good. US phones aren't compatible, however. There are relatively few **internet cafés** on Madeira. Possibly the best is **Cremesoda Cyber Café**, Rua Dos Ferreiros 9 (behind Igreja do Colegio),

Funchal, tel: 291 224 920, fax: 291 222 667. Open Monday–Friday 09:00–21:00, Saturday 10:00–21:00, Sunday 17:00–21:00, website: www.cremesoda.com

Electricity
The power supply is 220 volts AC. Sockets are 2-pin.

Weights and Measures
Madeira uses metric weights and measurements, and European clothing sizes.

GOOD READING

Cossart, N (1984) *Madeira the Island Vineyard*, Christie's Wine Publications, London.
Farrow, John and Susan (1990) *Madeira, the Complete Guide* (2nd edition), Robert Hale, London.
Liddell, Alex (1998) *Madeira*, Faber and Faber Ltd., London.
Monterey, Guido de (1998) *Madeira, Isle of Flowers* (4th edition), Jarmelos Criadores Distribuidores Graficos, Porto.
Moore, CC; Elias, G; Costa, H (1997) *Bird Watcher's Guide to Portugal and Madeira*, Prion Ltd.
Underwood, John and Pat (1999) *Landscapes of Madeira. A Countryside Guide* (5th edition). Sunflower Books, London.
Most American and English national **newspapers** are available, also a wide range of **magazines** in English. There are two island newspapers: *Jornal da Madeira* and *Diário de Notícias do Funchal*. The latter has a daily supplement in English, which includes details of TV and radio programmes in other languages.

Health Precautions
It is possible to burn very quickly in the Madeiran sun. Wear sunblock and if you are going to be out for a long time, cover exposed parts of your body. Tap water is safe to drink and tastes fresh. Mineral water is also widely available.

Health Services:
A visit to a doctor has to be paid for, so it's worth checking out the pharmacy first. Chemists are allowed to prescribe suitable medication – many speak a little English. If you're on medication, take supplies with you as your regular brand may not be available on the island.
In an emergency, the main **hospital** for foreigners is in Funchal: Cruz de Carvalho, Avenida Luis Camões, tel: 291 705 600. EU citizens should have their EHIC card to obtain a refund on basic treatment, and insurance that covers medical emergencies is also advisable for all visitors. There are many English-speaking doctors on Madeira – enquire at your hotel for details. Information about dental services in Funchal is available from hotels and tourist offices.

Personal Safety
Crime on Madeira is rare, but take the usual precautions. Deposit spare money and other valuables in the hotel safe. Do not leave valuables on the beach, at the poolside or in the car, and beware of the risk of pickpocketing in crowds. If you are the victim of theft, report it to the police and ask for a copy of the report if you intend to make an insurance claim.
The main **police station** is on Rua da Infância 28, tel: 291 222 022.
Lost Property is at Rua da Infância 28, tel: 291 208 200. If your passport goes missing you will need to get a replacement from your consulate:
UK, Rua da Alfandega, 10/3C, Funchal, tel: 291 212 600/7
USA, Rua da Alfandega, 10/2AB, Funchal, tel: 291 235 636.
South Africa, Praça António Nobre, Funchal, tel: 291 223 521, fax: 291 227 314.

Emergencies
Fire, **Ambulance** and **Police**: tel: 112.
Hospital Cruz Carvalho, Funchal, tel: 291 705 600.
Centro de Saúde do Porto Santo, tel: 291 982 361.

Etiquette
When greeting people they know, women kiss on both cheeks, men shake hands. Dress is informal, though after dark smart-casual clothing is generally worn. Topless sunbathing is permitted in the lidos and hotel pools.

Language
Portuguese is the language of Madeira but many people working with tourists speak English, and German too. Portuguese is easier to read than to speak (especially if you know some Spanish). Madeirans will, however, appreciate any effort you make to speak their language.

INDEX

Note: Numbers in **bold** indicate photographs

accommodation 58, 77, 95, 113, 121, 123
Adegas de São Francisco 5, 33, 39–40
Aquapark 106
aquarium 39
Archada do Pereira 94
architecture 61, 64, **107**
 Manueline 36, 42, 44, **46**, 65, 66, **67**, 105, 107
Arco do São Jorge 93–94
Avenida Arriaga 42–44
Avenida das Comunidades Madeirenses see Avenida do Mar
Avenida do Mar 44
azulejos **13**, **18**, 38, 43, 63, 74, 108

Balcões 9, 79, 87
beaches 5, 6, 61, 63, 67, 68, 72, 81, 82, 94, 104, 105, 111, 118, 120
 Calheta 6, **64**
 Machico 97, 108
 Porto Santo 5, 6, **114**, 115–116, **117**
 Praia da Barreirinha 51
 Praia Formosa 54
bird life 9–10
bird park see Jardim dos Loiros
boat trips 34, 44, 47, 61, 66, 77, 111, 115, 116, 120, 113, 121, 124
Boaventura 28, 79, 93
Boca da Corrida 76
Boca da Encumeada 7, 34, 61, 76
braguinha 21, 27
business hours 125

Cabeço Furado 89
Cabo Girão 5, **7**, 9, 17, 34, 64, 66, 79, 82, **83**–84
Caldeirão Verde 75, 93
Calheta 6, 16, 63, **64**–65, 69, 72, 74, 75
Calheta Marina 64
Camacha 28, 97, 100–101
Câmara de Lobos **20**, 66, 72, 79, **81**–83
Câmara Municipal 48
Caminho do Monte 79, 85–**86**
Caniçal 25, 44, 104, 107, 109, **110**, **111**
Caniço 55, 97, 105–106

Caniço de Baixo 97, 105, **106**, 111, 112
car rally 56
Casa das Queimadas 75, 92
Casa de Calçada 38
Casa de Portela 103, 104
Casa do Turista 44
Casa Sardinhas 112
cathedrals, chapels, churches and convents
 Arco da Calheta **65**
 Calheta parish church 64
 Caniço church 105
 Capela de Nossa Senhora da Conceição **82**
 Capela de Nossa Senhora de Piedade 111
 Capela de San Roque 72
 Capela do Corpo Santo 51
 Capela dos Milagres 107, 108
 Chapel of St Catherine **42**
 Chapel of Nossa Senhora da Graça 118
 Chapel of the Mother of God 105
 Chapel of the Three Kings 65
 Church of Our Lady of Monte 26, **78**, 79, 86
 Church of São Bento 66, **67**
 Convento de Santa Clara (Convent of St Clare) 33, **34**–35, 38, 46, 84
 Igreja do Colégio (Church of St John the Evangelist) 47
 Igreja do Socorro 51
 Igreja Inglesa (English Church) 36–**37**, 52
 Madalena do Mar 64
 Morgada chapel 116
 Nossa Senhora da Conceição 107
 Nossa Senhora da Luz 63
 Nossa Senhora da Piedade 111
 Ponta Delgada Church **93**, 94
 Santa Cruz parish church 66, 106
 São Jorge **94**
 São Pedro **38**
 São Roque 107
 São Vicente parish church 72
 Sé (Funchal Cathedral) 33, 42, 39, 45–**46**, 65, 66, 101
 St Sebastian parish church 82
Centro de Artes das Mudas 64

Chão de Ribeira 70
Christ the King (statue) 74, **104**, 105
Cidade Vila Baleira 115–117, 118, 120
climate 10–12
clothing 122–123
 Madeiran hats **28**
Columbus, Christopher 12, **14**, 16, 41, 45, 79, 115, 116–117
communications 125–126
Cristo Rei (statue) see Christ the King (statue)
Curral das Freiras 5, 34, 76, 79, **84**–85
Curral dos Romeiros 100
currency 123
customs 122
cycling 54

Desert Islands see Ilhas Desertas
drinks **31**

Eagle's Nest see Penha de Águia
economy 24–25
Eira do Serrado 84
electricity 123
embroidery 24, 27–29, 44, 51, 88
emergencies 126
Encumeada see Boca da Encumeada
Engenho da Calheta 69
espada **29**, 33, 81, 82
Estreito da Câmara de Lobos 82
estufalgem 40
etiquette 126
European Union 24–25

fado music 27
Faial 79, **89**, 118
Fajã do Nogueira 100
Fanal 68, 70–71
festivals **26**–27, 43, **45**, 48, 58, 62, 77, 82, 85, **91**, 92, 94, 95, 113, 123
fishing 5, 41, 59, 97, 106, 108, **109**, 116
flag **22**
flora 7–8, **9**, 22, 44, 70
flowers 5, 8, 36, 48, **49**, 53, 56–57, 87, 88, 99
folk costume **4**, **26**, 27
folk dancers **4**, **26**, 27, 92
folk music 26–27, 43, 68, 88, 101
Fonte da Areia 115, 117–118, 119
food **29**–30

football 50, 57, 106
Fortaleza de São Tiago 51, **52**
Forte do Nossa Senhora do Amparo 108
Franco, Francisco 23, 42, 43, 52
fruits **11**, 12, 30, 69, 90, 91
Funchal 5, **32**, 33–59, 104
Funchal Harbour **40**, 41–42
Furnas das Amasiadas 120

Galo Mar 104
Garajau 97, 111
Garajau natural marine park see Reserva Natural Parcial do Garajau
golf 5, 97, 98, 99, **102**, 105, 118
government 6, 23
Grupo Folclórico da Camacha 26, 101
Grutas de São Vicente 61, 73

health 122, 126
helicopter trips 41, 59, 83
history 13–23
holidays 123
horse riding 46, 50, 59
Hospício da Princesa 19, 42

Ilhas Desertas 7, 120
Ilhéu de Baixo 117
Ilhéu do Farol 112
Institute of Embroidery, Tapestry and Handicrafts (IBTAM) 51–52

Jardim Botânico 33, 34, 56–**57**
Jardim da Serra 83
Jardim de São Francisco 43, 44
Jardim do Mar 61, 65
Jardim do Monte Palace **13**, 86
Jardim dos Loiros 57
Jardim Orquídea 55, 57

Lamaceiros 89, 103
 water house 103
landscape 6–7, **10**, **73**, **90**
language 6, 10, 25, 30, 125, 126
Larano 105
Largo do Municipio 107
Largo do Pelourinho 116
Largo dos Milagros 108
Lazareto Quay 105
levadas 5, 12, 16

INDEX

Levada do Caldeirão 92
Levada do Furado 79, 88, 103
Levada do Portela 89, 103
Levada do Risco 75
Levada do Rocha Vermelha 75
Levada de Serra do Faial 103
Levada dos 25 Fontes 75
Levada dos Tornos **100**
Levada Nova 109
levada walking 12, 61, 63, 74, 75, 76, 79, 87
Living Science Centre 68

Machico **96**, 97, 104, 105, 107–**109**
Machico valley 97
Machin, Robert 109
Madalena do Mar 64, 104
Madeira International Airport **21**, 24, 25, 122
Madeira Magic 53
Madeira Story Centre 23, 33, 35, 51, 88
Madeira Theme Park 93
Madeira Wine Co 39–41
Madeira Wine Institute 49, 52
Mãe de Deus 105
Marina de Lugar de Baixo 63
Mercado dos Lavradores (Workers' Market) 33, 49–**50**, 55, 90
Miradouro dos Balcões 89
Miradouro dos Ingleses 102
Molhe da Pontinha 41
Monte 5, 34, 79, **85**–87
Monte Palace Tropical Garden *see* Jardim do Monte Palace
Morenos 115, 120
Municipal Garden *see* Jardim de São Francisco
Municipal Theatre 43
museums
 Casa Museu Frederico de Freitas 18, 37–**38**
 Christopher Columbus House Museum 116–117
 Ethnographical Museum *see* Museu Etnográfico da Madeira
 Museu da Baleia 110
 Museu de Arte Sacra 27, 33, 47, **48**, 64
 Museu do Instituto do Vinho da Madeira 48–49
 Museu Etnográfico da Madeira 67
 Museu Henrique e Francisco Franco 52

museums (cont.)
 Museu Municipal 38–39
 Museu Photographia Vicentes 36
Museum of Contemporary Art 51
Museum of Sacred Art *see* Museu de Arte Sacra
Natural History Museum 56
Núcleo Museológico 'A Cidade do Açúcar' 44
Quinta das Cruzes Museum 20, 36
Whaling Museum *see* Museu da Baleia
music 26–27, 43, 45, 50, 88, 101

North Coast Road **71**
Nossa Senhora da Conceição 41

O Relógio 101, **101**
Old Customs House 33, 44
Our Lady of Peace (statue) **17**, 87–**88**

Palácio de São Lourenço 33, 42–43, **44**
Palácio São Pedro *see* Museu Municipal
Palheiros 91, **92**
Parque de Santa Catarina 41–42, 44, 46, 48, 52, 73–74, **75**
Paúl do Mar 61, 65
Penha de Águia 89, 91, **103**, 104
people 25–31
Pico das Pedras 92
Pico das Pedras National Park 79, 80, 92
Pico dos Torres 82, 89
Pico de Ana Ferreira 120
Pico de Serradinho 76
Pico do Arieiro 5, 79, 90
Pico do Castelo 115, 119–120
Pico do Facho **98**, 108, 109
Pico do Facho, Porto Santo 115, 120
Pico do Suna 89
Pico dos Barcelos 54
Pico Grande 76
Pico Ruivo de Santana 6, 7, 90
Ponta da Calheta 117, 120
Ponta da Oliveira 105
Ponta de São Lourenço 9, 10, 34, 44, 97, 98, 102, 109, 111–**112**

Ponta Delgada 79, 94, 104
Ponta do Garajau **104**, 105
Ponta do Pargo **60**, 61, 62–**63**, 64
Ponta do Sol 47, 61, 63, 64, 74, 104
Ponta do Tristão 68
Ponta Pequena 65
Portela 97, **103**
Portela, Porto Santo 118
Porto da Cruz 89, **103**, 104–105
Porto Moniz 61, 67–**68**, 69, 71, 72, 104
Porto Santo 5, 6, 7, 9, 10, 11, 12, 41, 42, 54, 104, **114**, 115–**120**, 121
Porto Santo Golfe 118
pousada 90, 123
Praça do Municipio 46–**47**
Praia das Palmeiras 104
Prainha 104, 111

quintas 71
 Quinta Bela Vista 47
 Quinta da Boa Vista 53, 55
 Quinta das Cruzes 16, **19**, 33, 35–**36**, 42, 66, 71
 Quinta de Bom Successo 56
 Quinta do Arco 93
 Quinta do Jardim da Serra 52, 83
 Quinta do Monte 71, 86, 87
 Quinta do Palheiro Ferreiro 5, 71, 97, 98–99
 Quinta do Santo da Serra 102
 Quinta Magnólia 54, 71, 104
 Quinta Vigia 42, 71

Rabaçal 7, 61, 74–75
Reid's Palace Hotel **55**
religion 6, 26
Reserva Natural Parcial do Garajau 105, **106**, 112
restaurants 58–59, 77, 95, 113, 121, 123
Ribeira Brava 7, 44, 47, 61, 66–**67**, 76
Ribeira da Fonte do Louro 92
Ribeira da Metade valley 79, 89
Ribeira do Pôrco 79, 93
Ribeira dos Cedros 92
Ribeira Grande 92
Ribeira São Vicente 7
Ribeira Seca 91, 109

Ribeiro Frio 75, 79, 88–**89**
Ribeiro São Jorge 100

safety 126
Santa Cruz 66, 97, 104, 106
 Law Courts 106, **107**
Santana **8**, 80, 91–93
Santo da Serra 97, 101–102
São Jorge 94
São Vicente 6, 61, **70**, 72–73, **74**
scuba diving 5, 63, 97, 105, 106, 112
Seixal 68–70
Selvagens 7, 22
Senhor Bom Jesus 94
Serra de Água **76**
Serra de Dentro 118–119
Serra de Fora 118, 120
shopping 33, 55, 59, 67, 88, 108, 120
soccer *see* football
Sports Park 106
swimming 51, 54, 55, 63, **69**, 94, 104, **106**, 108, 111

telephones 125
Terreiro da Luta **17**, 85, 87
time 125
toboggans 5, 67, 79, 85, **87**
tourist offices 59, 77, 95, 113, 121, 122
tours 59, 77, 95, 113
Toyota car showroom **43**
transport 59, 77, 85, 95, 113, 121, 124
Tropical Garden *see* Caminho do Monte

Veitch, Henry 19, 20, 21, 37, 49, 52, 83
Vila Baleira *see* Cidade Vila Baleira
visas 122
volcanoes 6, 73

websites 9
whaling 107, 110, **111**
wickerwork 24, 28, 44, 67, 88, 97, 100–**101**
windmills 118, 120
wine 5, 14, **16**–17, 31, 33, 39–41, 49, 69, 70, **72**, 82, 88, 93, 104, 116

Zarco, João Gonçalves 13, 14, **23**, 33, 34, 35, 36, 42, 48, 52, 54, **66**, 81, 97, 107, 109, 118
Zimbralinho 120
Zona Velha 33, 44, 50–53